FINANCIAL STATECRAFT

Benn Steil and Robert E. Litan

FINANCIAL STATECRAFT

THE ROLE OF FINANCIAL MARKETS IN AMERICAN FOREIGN POLICY

A COUNCIL ON FOREIGN RELATIONS / BROOKINGS INSTITUTION BOOK

Yale University Press
New Haven and London

A COUNCIL ON FOREIGN RELATIONS / BROOKINGS INSTITUTION BOOK

Published with assistance from the Mary Cady Tew Memorial Fund.

Set in Galliard type by SPI Publisher Services.
Printed in the United States of America.

Library of Congress Cataloging-in-Publication Data
Steil, Benn.
    Financial statecraft: The role of financial markets in American foreign policy / Benn Steil and Robert E. Litan.
        p. cm.
    "A Council on Foreign Relations / Brookings Institution Book."
    Includes bibliographical references and index.
    ISBN-13: 978-0-300-10975-7 (alk. paper)
    ISBN-10: 0-300-10975-X (alk. paper)
1. Financial institutions—United States. 2. Capital movements—Government policy—United States. 3. United States—Foreign relations. 4. International finance. 5. International relations.
I. Litan, Robert E., 1950- II. Title.
    HG181.S797 2006
    332'.0424—dc22

                                                2005012039

A catalogue record for this book is available from the British Library.

The paper in this book meets the guidelines for permanence and durability of the Committee on Production Guidelines for Book Longevity of the Council on Library Resources.

10 9 8 7 6 5 4 3 2 1

The Council on Foreign Relations

Founded in 1921, the Council on Foreign Relations is an independent, national membership organization and a nonpartisan center for scholars dedicated to producing and disseminating ideas so that individual and corporate members, as well as policymakers, journalists, students, and interested citizens in the United States and other countries, can better understand the world and the foreign policy choices facing the United States and other governments. The Council does this by convening meetings; conducting a wide-ranging Studies program; publishing *Foreign Affairs,* the preeminent journal covering international affairs and U.S. foreign policy; maintaining a diverse membership; sponsoring Independent Task Forces; and providing up-to-date information about the world and U.S. foreign policy on the Council's website, www.cfr.org.

The Brookings Institution

The Brookings Institution is an independent organization devoted to nonpartisan research, education, and publication in economics, governance, foreign policy, and the social sciences generally. Its principal purposes are to aid in the development of sound public policies and to promote public understanding of issues of national importance. The Institution was founded on December 8, 1927, to merge the activities of the Institute for Government Research, founded in 1916, the Institute of Economics, founded in 1922, and the Robert Brookings Graduate School of Economics and Government, founded in 1924. The Institution maintains a position of neutrality on issues of public policy. Interpretations or conclusions in Brookings publications should be understood to be solely those of the authors.

CONTENTS

ACKNOWLEDGMENTS

Having endeavored to cover a wide intellectual terrain in this book, we are heavily indebted to six extremely bright, able, and motivated young men for the critical research support they provided: Michael Punzalan, James Bergman, Jesse Gurman, Daren Tedeschi, Erik Daly, and Hallvard Omholt. We were also privileged to have had the sage advice and criticism of an extraordinary Council on Foreign Relations study group and would like to express our warmest thanks to each of the members who so generously dedicated their time and shared their expertise with us: Peter Baird, John Biggs, Lael Brainard, Domingo Cavallo, Joyce Chang, Saj Cherian, Blair Effron, Mallory Factor, Tom Farmer, Sergio Galvis, Anna Gelpern, Jon Hartzell, Manuel Hinds, Gary Hufbauer, Peter Kenen, John Lipsky, Karin Lissakers, David Malpass, Michael Moskow, Ernie Patrikis, Adam Posen, Paul Sacks, Frank Savage, Brad Setser, Dan Tarullo, Ted Truman, and, in particular, the chairman of the group, Jeff Shafer. We further benefited from the detailed comments of three anonymous referees and from a number of extended private interviews with some key players in American financial statecraft over the past decade, and we are grateful for their time and candid insights. We are also grateful for the financial support of Harry Freeman. Finally, we would like to thank Jack Ferrer at JP Morgan's ADR.com and Nadav Glucklich at Thomson Financial for their invaluable assistance in identifying and providing important investment data referred to in the text. Of course, all errors and other failings are ours, and ours alone.

1

(WHAT IS FINANCIAL STATECRAFT?)

As long as the world remains divided into sovereign nations, there will always be a need for statecraft—the means by which governments pursue foreign policy. Harold Lasswell (1958), one of the scholarly giants in this field, suggested that statecraft was pursued through four primary instruments: information (words and propaganda), diplomacy (negotiations and deals), force (weapons and violence), and economics (goods and money).[1] The scholarly literature on foreign policy is full of major treatises, articles, and other texts on the first three of these instruments. There remains, however, a single classic text on "economic statecraft." Though in his book by that title, David Baldwin (1985) provides no single, all-encompassing definition of the term, one can be spliced together from his discussions of both statecraft and economics: Economic statecraft encompasses efforts by governments to influence other actors in the international system, relying primarily on resources that have "a reasonable semblance of a market price in terms of money."[2] Baldwin's reference to money prices is intended to distinguish economic statecraft from other types of statecraft, such as military statecraft, which utilize nonpecuniary means of persuasion or coercion, while at the same time accommodating the broadest possible range of measures that could usefully be called economic.

Economic statecraft has become increasingly important in the post–World War II era, as trade in goods and services has expanded robustly. The widened flow of trade has encouraged governments—

notably, but not exclusively, the United States—to try to use their power over what can be imported into and exported from their countries as a lever, short of war, to influence the behavior of other governments.

Economic statecraft is not the same as foreign economic policy. Economic statecraft applies economic means to ends which may or may not be economic, whereas foreign economic policy encompasses means which may or may not be economic in the service of economic ends.[3] Thus, trade sanctions imposed on a country in order to persuade it to halt a weapons program would qualify as economic statecraft, but not foreign economic policy, whereas suspending certain diplomatic contacts with a country—a noneconomic intervention—in order to protest its import barriers would qualify as foreign economic policy, but not economic statecraft. The distinction is important for us, as we focus here specifically on the use of *economic means* in the service of *both economic and traditional foreign policy ends.*)

The most common and widely studied tool of economic statecraft is economic sanctions, particularly trade sanctions. Meghan O'Sullivan, in the New Testament of sanctions texts, *Smart Sanctions* (2003), defines sanctions as "the deliberate withdrawal of normal trade or financial relations for foreign policy purposes."[4] The effectiveness of sanctions in terms of achieving foreign policy ends has been the subject of tremendous, and often heated, debate among both policymakers and scholars. Successful sanctions, as we will see in our own examination of capital markets sanctions in chapter 4, are often in the eye of the beholder, in the sense that the symbolic significance of sending nonviolent messages of political displeasure and, perhaps, of being willing to resort to more coercive forms of pressure in the future is often prized wholly irrespective of whether end-goals are actually achieved directly through their use. But if the achievement of such end-goals is to be the touchstone, O'Sullivan's assessment speaks for nearly two decades of scholarly literature. Her case studies "not only confirm the much-heralded conclusion that multilateral sanctions are the most effective form of economic pressure, but also suggest that even targeted or limited multilateral measures are preferable to comprehensive, unilateral ones."[5]

But trade is not the only way in which nations interact with each other economically. Whereas influencing international trade flows has long been and continues to be an important political objective and tool, another form of international economic exchange has risen to a level of much greater macroeconomic significance and political concern over the past two decades. This is the purchase and sale of financial assets—such as bonds, stocks, and derivative contracts—across borders, an activity whose growth has vastly outpaced that of traditional trade. Nearly $2 trillion worth of currency now moves cross-border everyday, roughly 90 percent of which is accounted for by financial flows unrelated to trade in goods and services—a stunning inversion of the figures in 1970, when 90 percent of international transactions were accounted for by trade.[6]

The relative importance of trade in goods and services, on the one hand, and trade in financial assets, on the other, is clearly illustrated in the U.S. balance of payments figures. If we chart the sum of American imports and exports (current account items) side by side with the sum of

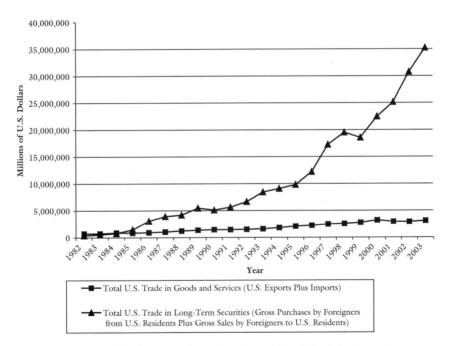

Figure 1. U.S. Total Trade in Goods and Services vs. Total Trade in Long-Term Securities. Source: Bureau of Economic Analysis; United States Department of the Treasury.

American foreign securities purchases and domestic securities sales to for-eigners (capital account items), we see dramatically more rapid growth in the latter since the mid-1980s.

The answer to the question, "Why did Willie Sutton rob banks?"—because that's where the money is—captures precisely why governments have increasingly turned to banks and other financial institutions as objects and instruments of foreign policy. In the mid-1990s, after the cus-tomary lag required for politics to catch up with economics, the arsenal of economic statecraft began expanding in response to the growing importance of financial flows. Both the Clinton administration and its Republican opponents in Congress began to focus on how control of financial market institutions, instruments, and practices could be applied in the service of foreign policy—with the two sides often reaching very different conclusions.

The time is ripe, therefore, to ask some fundamental questions about the emergence of what we call here financial statecraft. *We identify as financial statecraft those aspects of economic statecraft that are directed at influencing capital flows.* These efforts have frequently involved harness-ing financial institutions to achieve certain foreign policy objectives. But precisely how has the American government practiced financial statecraft? How effective have these efforts been? And how could they be made more effective? These are the central questions we tackle in this book.

To illustrate the nature of our task, and how economic statecraft differs from financial statecraft, we consider below some traditional forms of eco-nomic statecraft and their much more recent financial statecraft counterparts:

Economic Statecraft	*Financial Statecraft*
Trade privileges, tariffs, and quotas	Capital flow guarantees and restrictions
Trade sanctions on states	Financial sanctions on nonstate actors
Foreign aid in drought or disaster	Underwriting foreign debt in a currency crisis
Regional trade agreements	Currency unions or dollarization

The right-hand list is qualitatively different from the left-hand one in that each of the items on the right involves a manifestly greater degree of political sensitivity or "sovereign intrusion." To be specific:

- Capital flows can have a vastly more immediate and dramatic influence than trade flows not only over movements in the relative value of national currencies but on the most basic economic and political conditions in a country.
- Threats of U.S. financial sanctions on foreign companies doing business with states subject to U.S. economic sanctions invariably provoke heated objections from foreign governments, which view them as overtly hostile acts and illegitimately extra-territorial in their reach.
- Bailouts of indebted foreign governments routinely provoke cries from around the world against the harshness of the conditionality applied, while at the same time calling forth condemnation of the moral hazard injected into international lending.
- The abolition of a national currency involves a major ceding of governmental control over national economic conditions to foreign bodies and is effectively irreversible without incurring significant economic and political turmoil.

In short, the stakes are higher and the foreign policy challenges are greater and more complex for financial statecraft than for traditional economic statecraft. Furthermore, policymakers frequently apply financial statecraft with a poor understanding of how financial markets actually work, leading to policy actions which are inadequate or which exacerbate the problems they are trying to remedy. Neither the phenomenon of financial statecraft nor its connection with the growth of financial flows, however, has received any systematic scholarly treatment.

This is a gap we hope to fill in the chapters that follow. Our objectives are both positive and normative. We aim to illuminate the relationship between financial flows and traditional foreign policy concerns, and the way in which the American government has attempted to harness financial markets and institutions in the service of foreign policy goals. We also aim to offer suggestions for change; sometimes very dramatic change. We believe that much of what is currently both integral to and absent from financial statecraft is based on dangerous but widespread misdiagnoses. Financial statecraft has a checkered past: some successes, and many more failures. There are also inherent limits to how successful financial statecraft can be in some settings. Where governments can usefully test those limits, we suggest how; and where they cannot, we suggest that the attempt not be made.

The first half of this book, chapters 2–4, examines the microeconomic aspects of financial statecraft, those focused on the specific institutions comprising the financial markets. The U.S. government has over the past 30 years attempted, sometimes alternatingly, sometimes simultaneously, to encourage as well as assist U.S. financial institutions in doing business overseas, on the one hand, and to restrain their ability to do so, on the other. Policy toward financial institutions has been driven in one direction by mercantilist motivations, in another by fears of risky global overstretch, and in yet another by a perceived need to enlist them in global wars, such as those on drugs and terror. The tremendous growth and internationalization of the U.S. markets for equity and bond finance in the 1990s has further led to increasingly vocal and influential calls to add denial of access to U.S. capital markets to America's arsenal of economic sanctions. All of these efforts, we argue, require significant recalibration to take better account of how financial markets work and how cost-effective these efforts are in achieving the foreign policy aims that motivate them.

The second half of this book, chapters 5–7, examines the macroeconomic aspects of financial statecraft, those focused more broadly on cross-border capital flows. As more and more countries around the world have chosen to enter the burgeoning global dollar-dominated marketplace for capital, national and regional financial crises have become more and more commonplace. As we demonstrate, these developments have raised significant new foreign policy challenges for the United States. New policy thinking is therefore needed. A new model must recognize that governments and companies around the world will continue to import capital prodigiously for the same sound economic reasons that U.S. regions import capital from other U.S. regions. Yet imports of capital by countries whose currencies are not, in turn, wanted abroad can lead to dangerous currency mismatch in their national balance sheets. Financial crises, therefore, will continue to occur in the absence of significant policy changes—particularly those related specifically to currency—in these countries as well as in the United States.

The workings of financial markets are frequently complex and growing increasingly important to the performance of national economies and political systems. This is why discussion and debate on the issues highlighted in this book are so important. Some of our analysis will be controversial; some will perhaps even appear counterintuitive. In particular, readers will discover as they proceed that tradeoffs are inherent in financial statecraft. Financial statecraft is also complicated in large part because money moves across jurisdictions so fast and in such large volumes that it, and the institutions that handle it, are difficult to redirect—it is frequently like trying to catch mercury. Moreover, steering financial markets in the service of foreign policy ends can have, and has at times had, economic costs both at home and abroad. For all these reasons, the wisdom of engaging in or forswearing financial statecraft is not determinable in the abstract.

Nonetheless, the cost-benefit calculus can and should be much more clearly illuminated in each particular case than it has been to date; both to improve it through a better political decision-making process where possible, and simply to improve the outcomes of the decision-making process where it is not. These are the aims of this book.

I

OF BANKS AND BOMBS

2

BANKING AND FOREIGN POLICY

Winning a war is the most monumental challenge any national leader can face. For Abraham Lincoln, one of the most vexing challenges posed by the American Civil War was figuring out how to pay for it.[1] His Treasury secretary, Salmon Chase, initially followed the strategy used by European monarchs in the seventeenth and eighteenth centuries, issuing $150 million in bonds to domestic banks. But since these bonds were then sold to British banks, this strategy put the Union at the mercy of a foreign power sympathetic to the Confederacy. Lincoln therefore changed course, following a plan developed by Chase, and effectively drafted the banks into the war. In December 1861, Lincoln submitted to Congress a bill that would require nationally chartered banks to deposit with the Treasury government bonds equal to at least one-third of their capital. Congress adopted the plan in 1863.[2]

As we will see in this and the subsequent chapter, banks continue to this day to be used by governments as a tool to fight wars and pursue foreign policy. And in the 1980s and 1990s, as banking became a truly global business, banks became *objects* of foreign policy, through the development of international financial regulations to promote prudence in risk taking, vigilance in customer monitoring, and a semblance of parity in cross-border competition. At the same time, governments have frequently deferred to or sought to promote the narrow interests of banks (and other financial institutions) in international regulatory and trade initiatives. The results have been decidedly mixed.

Banks, OPEC, and Petrodollar Recycling: Beginnings of a New Financial Statecraft

There have been certain defining years in postwar economic history, and 1973 was undoubtedly one of them. That was the year the era of cheap energy ended. Angered by U.S. support for Israel during the October 1973 "Yom Kippur" war, the Arab members of the Organization of Petroleum Exporting Countries (OPEC) struck back, embargoing oil exports to the United States and enforcing that dramatic step by agreeing to cut production dramatically. The reduced supply led to much higher oil prices—from a prewar $3 per barrel to a postwar $12 per barrel. By one estimate at the time, the price increase added $37 billion to the cost of petroleum products in the United States,[3] which in turn caused prices of other energy sources to jump as well. The result was a new phenomenon that afflicted the United States and oil-importing countries throughout the world: stagflation, the combination of slow growth or recession with sharply higher inflation.

OPEC countries didn't suffer, however. Between 1972 and 1974, annual oil revenues of OPEC countries rose from $14 billion to nearly $70 billion. By 1977, OPEC oil revenues had reached $128 billion.[4]

What did the OPEC countries do with all this cash? By 1981, they had put three-fourths of their surplus into industrialized countries, one-quarter in the United States alone.[5] Some of the Saudi government's investments, in particular, were placed in U.S. Treasury bonds, in response to secret solicitations by U.S. government officials.[6] This outcome was ironic, to say the least, given that the United States was the principal target of OPEC's production cutback and price hike. Much of the rest of the OPEC surplus, though, was stashed away in large U.S. and foreign banks.

What did the *banks* do with all the OPEC money? The U.S. economy was then mired in recession—largely because of the OPEC oil price hike—and many consumers and businesses did not want to borrow; many of those who did had questionable credit. As for the safest borrowers, large corporations, they had over time been issuing more and more commercial paper (short-term debt instruments) directly to large institutional buyers, such as pension funds and insurance companies, rather than borrowing more expensively from banks. Where else could the banks put this money to use?

The short answer is that the banks rediscovered lending to less developed countries (LDCs), their governments in particular. We say "rediscovered" because LDCs were a favorite destination of U.S. bond investors in the run-up to the Great Depression. Those investments, not surprisingly, did not turn out well. But a new generation of bankers who had not lived through that searing experience were ready to try again, eager for the fatter margins they believed they could earn by lending to LDC governments.

There is evidence that the banks got some friendly advice, and perhaps some subtle pressure, from U.S. government officials, who feared that if the institutions did not "recycle" the OPEC surplus into the developing world, not only those countries would suffer but so would the United States and other industrialized countries which exported to LDCs. As one of President Gerald Ford's top economic advisers, Bill Seidman, candidly admitted well after he had left his position, "The entire Ford Administration, including me, told the large banks that the process of recycling petrodollars to the less developed countries was beneficial, *and perhaps a patriotic duty*" (emphasis added).[7]

And lend they did, especially to governments in Latin America. By mid-1982, U.S. bank claims to their southern neighbors totaled $82.5 billion, or one-fourth of all foreign claims by U.S. banks at the time.[8] The nine largest U.S. banks provided nearly two-thirds of this lending.[9] Despite the encouragement of some U.S. policymakers, others were nervous about the heavy lending by banks to sovereign government borrowers in the developing world. Congress began holding hearings about the issue as early as 1975. In 1977, a staff report issued by the Senate Subcommittee on Foreign Relations worried openly that bank lending to these governments threatened the "stability of the U.S. banking system and by extension the international financial system."[10] Even the chairman of the Federal Reserve, Arthur Burns, criticized the banks in April 1977 for extending too much to countries that were too much in debt.[11] But at the White House, the concerns voiced by Burns (and Congress) were dismissed. The economic needs of the nation, or even of the world, trumped hand-wringing about bank safety. Again, as Seidman forthrightly admits, "We just did not see the magnitude of the trouble ahead. We saw only the short-term benefits of the loans to our industry and finance. But then, long-range planning has never been an outstanding attribute of our governmental process."[12]

The warnings of the Cassandras fell on deaf ears. Banks continued to lend. Then came another oil price earthquake in late 1978, when oil traders helped push prices to $40 a barrel in the wake of the Iranian revolution.[13] The second oil price shock was a deep setback not only to the U.S. economy, but also to oil-importing developing economies that by the late 1970s were just beginning to get back on their feet. With much higher oil prices came the need for new rounds of financing. Where else to turn but to the banks that had financed them before?

Again, the banks were all too willing to respond. By 1982, the nine largest U.S. banks had extended a total of $83 billion to developing countries, $51 billion to Latin America alone. The banks' LDC exposure by then exceeded their official stated capital—shareholders' equity and retained earnings—by a ratio of almost three to one.

This time, there is little evidence that the banks were being pressured by policymakers. To the contrary, regulators strongly cautioned the banks about the dangers of their lending. By 1979, Federal Reserve Chairman Paul Volcker was worrying that rising oil prices would require the rescheduling of some debts already owed by developing countries.[14] In 1981, Volcker's highly respected Fed colleague, the former Yale professor Henry Wallich, urged regulators to restrain bank lending to LDCs because it put the capital of the core banks, in particular, in jeopardy.[15] Even the editorial writers of the *Wall Street Journal* were concerned, warning that the $500 billion of debt that the LDCs had run up "look[ed] starkly ominous, threatening a chain reaction of country defaults, bank failures and a general depression matching that of the 1930s."[16]

But, as they had with previous warnings, bankers brushed these cautions aside. One of the world's leading bankers at the time, Citicorp Chairman Walter Wriston, summed it all up when he pronounced that "countries don't go bankrupt."[17] Moreover, despite the worldwide recession that the second oil price shock had helped trigger, Wriston was upbeat about the prospects of the LDC economies: "One by one, we are seeing developing countries finally breaking through the vicious circle of poverty. Far from despairing, I have great hopes for the future of the LDCs in the remaining years of this century."[18]

As it turns out, some of the world's LDCs, notably China and India, eventually proved that they did have a bright future. But in the short run, Wriston's remark, uttered in 1981, could not have been more poorly timed. In 1982, Mexico, a large oil-*exporting* country, said it couldn't service its debts on their original terms. Other indebted countries soon announced they had similar problems. If they hadn't realized it before, it was clear now: the banks had an LDC debt crisis on their hands.

While the largest U.S. banks soon began doing everything they could to reduce their LDC debt exposures, they didn't want to recognize publicly the potential losses from these loans on their financial statements. If they had done that, they would have had to add significantly to their loan loss reserves, or even to write off some of the loans themselves. Either course would have eaten into retained earnings and thus into shareholders' equity. Although the markets effectively did this for them—by imposing steep discounts on their stock prices—the banks and their regulators kept up the fiction for most of the decade that the banks were going to be repaid. The fiction was evident from the bank's own financial statements, which reported shareholders' equity based on the book values of the bank loans. But the *market value* of the banks' equity was much lower.

For the rest of the eighties, banks and their LDC borrowers jockeyed for position. The banks were unwilling to provide new money, but also unwilling to forgive any of the old money they had already extended. By 1987, the banks' tenuous position was finally exposed when they began to set aside much larger reserves for losses on their LDC loans. In 1989, Treasury Secretary Nicholas Brady proposed a grand debt swap that resulted a year later in the banks' effectively forgiving a large part of their LDC debt, a step that many economists, such as Jeffrey Sachs, had been urging for some time.

In sum, what began as a subtle effort by the U.S. government to harness U.S. banks in helping to "save the world economy" in the mid-1970s became by the end of the 1980s an effort by the U.S. government to force those banks to recognize their excesses. The focus had shifted dramatically from promoting foreign lending to restraining it.

The Importance of Bank Capital

Banks are not like other firms in the economy. The typical non-banking firm finances itself through a combination of debt (bank loans or bonds) and equity (capital supplied by shareholders or owners and accumulated earnings of the firm). The debt of a typical nonbanking firm has a fixed maturity: the lender cannot ask for the funds back until the term of the loan (or the bond) is due.

This is not the case with banks. Banks obtain virtually all of their funds from depositors, who place their money in the bank for safekeeping and transactions. The largest portions of most banks' deposits are in demand accounts, which means that depositors can withdraw their money at any time. In contrast, most of the assets held by banks—loans—are illiquid; they cannot be turned into cash until they are due, and even then some are rolled over when the borrower doesn't have the cash to repay immediately.

In short, banks must live with what economists call a maturity mismatch: bank liabilities (deposits) tend to have much shorter maturities than do their assets (loans). Under normal circumstances, banks can live with this mismatch because of the fact that only a small number of their depositors will want to withdraw their money at any given point in time. This allows them safely to lend out most of their depositors' funds to borrowers for extended periods of time. Banks use the same principle to take advantage of much more leverage than the typical nonbanking firm. It has not been uncommon for shareholders' equity to back less than 10 percent of the bank's assets, far less than what is typical for a nonbanking firm. Using such leverage, banks can make money on the spread between the interest they pay depositors and the interest they receive from borrowers, without having to invest much of their owners' capital in the process.

But for the purposes of maintaining the safety and soundness of the financial system as a whole, it is important that banks have at least a minimum amount of capital, or "skin in the game." Otherwise, there is a risk that a jump in loan defaults during an economic downturn could cause banks to become insolvent: that is, their assets will not be sufficient to cover what they owe depositors. This risk can be especially worrisome if the government *insures* the deposits of banks, which the United States has done since the Great Depression and which many other countries have started doing in more recent years. In that event, the government insurer effectively becomes liable for all losses banks may suffer in excess of their capital. Knowing this, banks can be tempted to take too much risk at the government's expense. That is the lesson of the infamous savings and loan disaster in the United States during the 1980s. Depository institutions that were effectively insolvent at the beginning of the decade were allowed to remain open and to gamble for resurrection: if the risky, high-interest loans they extended were repaid, the institutions' owners would win, but if the loans turned sour, the government—and ultimately taxpayers—would lose. In the event, American taxpayers eventually picked up a tab of roughly $150 billion for loan gambles that turned out badly.

Accordingly, it is essential that governments closely watch over banks and other depository institutions or regulate them in some manner. In the United States, the states and the federal government (depending on which level of government grants the charter) have regulated banks in two ways: by limiting their activities (and their affiliations) and by trying to keep their capital from falling below a minimum fraction of their assets.

Financial Regulation as Financial Statecraft

Regulators originally took a case-by-case approach to supervising bank capital-to-asset ratios.[19] This changed in 1980, when the three U.S. bank regulators—the Federal Reserve, the Federal Deposit Insurance Corporation (FDIC), and the Comptroller of the Currency—issued capital-to-asset guidelines for banks to follow.[20] But Congress was not content with mere guidelines. It wanted harder rules. So in 1983, Congress enacted the International Lending Supervision Act, which, among other things, told regulators to set capital standards that could be enforced.

At the same time, Congress did not want the regulators to set new standards without ensuring competitive equality in international markets. Neither did Chairman Volcker. While he had previously admitted that politics had made it difficult to rein in the banks that were busy extending loans to LDC governments,[21] he told Congress, *"I cannot emphasize strongly enough our interest in the competitiveness of U.S. banks"* (emphasis added).[22] These concerns were not unfounded. Between 1973 and 1978, the number of foreign banks operating in the United States more than doubled, from 60 to 122, and their combined assets increased from $37 billion to $90 billion.[23]

Especially worrisome was the growing competitiveness of Japanese banks in the United States. Before 1980, the United States had primarily been host to European banks. But in the 1980s, Japanese banks began to make significant inroads into the U.S. banking market. In 1988, the 10 largest banks in the world, as measured by total assets, were all Japanese; by the early 1990s, Japanese banks accounted for 18 percent of U.S. commercial and industrial lending.[24] One reason these banks were able to grow so large is that Japanese bank regulators not only let them leverage lower capital-asset ratios than were required in other countries, but they also let the banks count so-called hidden reserves as part of their capital. Hidden reserves consisted of a portion of the increase in market value of the stocks they carried on their books. Since American banks were prohibited from using such accounting practices, they were at a significant competitive disadvantage. The fact that the biggest U.S. banks had large LDC credits outstanding did not help their position. It was clear that the playing field was far from level.

The pursuit of a level playing field drove bank capital regulation toward internationalization. It was, indeed, a new form of financial statecraft. The Federal Reserve initiated this process in consort with its British counterpart, the Bank of England, which had common concerns about bank capital positions at the time. The outcome was a new risk-based system of bank capital standards. Instead of simply requiring banks to back a fixed percentage of their assets with shareholders' funds, the new regime assigned risk weights to different asset types and then required bank capital to exceed a minimum percentage of the overall amount of weighted assets. Assets judged to have no risk, such as rich-country government bonds (those issued by governments belonging to the Organization for Economic Cooperation and Development, or OECD), were given a zero weight, while most other loans were given a 100 percent weight. With much fanfare, the regulators from the two countries agreed to this new risk-based system in 1986.

With the U.S.–U.K. bank capital accord under their belts, the Federal Reserve and the Comptroller of the Currency raised their sights, hoping to pull into the system banks from all rich countries, especially Japan. As it turns out, there was a ready-made forum for carrying out this vision: the Basel Committee on Banking Supervision, part of the multilateral Bank for International Settlements in Switzerland, which had been working on the idea of risk-based capital standards on its own for some time.

The Basel committee, consisting of central banks from 13 of the world's richest nations, was established at the end of 1974 to coordinate the supervision of internationally active banks. The need for supervision became apparent after the momentous failure of Germany's Bankhaus Herstatt. The bank, which owed dollars to banks around the world, sent shock waves through the international financial community when it collapsed. On its ruins, the foundations for international banking regulation were laid.

Given the work that the United States and Great Britain had put into their U.S.–U.K. risk-based capital accord, the Basel committee saved considerable effort by adopting most of the U.S.–U.K. accord as its own. In 1988, the committee established a risk-based system of capital standards built on four different "risk buckets," or categories of assets, with weights ranging from 0 to 100 percent to reflect their relative riskiness. From the American perspective, though, perhaps the most significant achievement of the accord was the fact that Japan had agreed to cease permitting its banks to count much of their hidden reserves in calculating their regulatory capital.[25] However, as we will see, this victory proved to be only temporary.

The Limits of Financial Regulation as Financial Statecraft

Though it was widely lauded by many commentators and rich-country banks at the time, the Basel Capital Accord was, in fact, deeply flawed. At best, it proved to be irrelevant when really needed. At worst, it led to some perverse results.[26]

The first problem did not take long to surface. Shortly after the Basel standards were finalized in late 1988, the United States and other countries fell into recession. Even without the Accord, banks would have adopted more cautious lending policies in that economic climate. Under the new Accord, the banks' caution in lending bordered on the ridiculous.[27] The problem was that the new risk-based formulae required banks to hold no capital against government bonds in their portfolios, but 4 percent "Tier 1" capital[28] against most loans. Reacting, in part, to these conditions, U.S. banks reduced their loans while increasing their holdings of Treasury bonds by nearly 50 percent between 1989 and 1992. The result was a credit crunch.

Other problems with the Basel standards were even more fundamental. While the system appropriately used a bank's capital-to-asset ratio to determine its risk of failure, the calculation of these ratios was overly simplistic. It involved summing up the amounts of capital required for different classes of bank assets and multiplying them by their individual risk weights. But it ignored a fundamental principle of financial economics: portfolios of assets benefit from *diversification*. That is, when the value of one asset goes up another might go down. In a diversified portfolio, the true risks of a portfolio of assets could very well be *less* than the risks measured by simply adding up the risks of each individual asset.

Furthermore, even on their own terms, the Basel risk weights were highly arbitrary. The accord made no effort to distinguish between the risks of different types of consumer and commercial loans, let alone assign presumably higher risk weights to loans to developing countries which happened to be OECD members, such as Mexico, whose borrowings had led to the bank capital problem in the first place. This shortcoming could allow some banks with especially risky loan portfolios to have the same levels of required capital as banks with less risky loan portfolios. This is not only unfair—it is an invitation to behave imprudently.

But the most fundamental flaw in the Basel Accord was that it contained no agreement on how to define and account for nonperforming loans—loans on which borrowers were not making timely payments of principal and interest. This was not just a technical omission; it was a huge loophole. Bank capital cannot be accurately measured unless the stated values of loans on a bank's balance sheet reflect their true worth. If the financial statements do not fully reflect the losses that banks are likely to incur on their loan portfolios, they will overstate both earnings and capital and thereby mask their shortfalls in capital. Countries that allow this accounting practice run higher risks of bank failure. Those that outlaw it put their banks at a competitive disadvantage. This, of course, was the dilemma Basel was supposed to prevent.

The ink was barely dry on the Accord before this problem became apparent. The triggering event was the collapse of the Japanese stock market in 1989 and the subsequent collapse of real estate prices in the country. Because real estate backed so many of the loans that Japanese banks had extended to their customers, many of these loans would probably not be fully repaid.[29] By any market-based test, most of the country's major banks had insufficient or even zero regulatory capital. But since they did not have to account for their nonperforming loans, they were able to mask their capital deficiencies. Like U.S. regulators in the 1980s, Japanese regulators feared that strictly enforcing capital standards and taking a tough position on the banks' nonperforming loans would push many banks close to or into insolvency. So the regulators looked the other way and hoped that land prices, stock prices, and economic activity would soon recover.[30]

But there was no recovery. The Japanese economy, stock market, and real estate market remained depressed throughout the 1990s. Many Japanese banks were in fact insolvent or nearly so, yet neither the Bank of Japan nor the Ministry of Finance wanted to recognize this fact officially and force any of the largest banks to close. Instead, throughout much of the 1990s, Japanese officials encouraged the large, weak banks to merge with one another in a tepid effort to consolidate operations and realize some minor cost savings (layoffs were excluded from the equation). At the same time, politicians encouraged the banks to continue lending to many troubled companies in an effort to keep the country from suffering a wave of bankruptcies. Eventually, Japanese regulators began a laudable effort to toughen their supervision and force banks to recognize losses on their nonperforming loans, but not before Japan suffered significant economic damage.

Japan is not the only country whose bank regulators looked the other way when times were tough. Since the advent of the Basel Accord, regulators in both France and Germany let certain of their larger banks continue to operate with insufficient capital ratios when they ran into trouble. Some countries, in contrast, took much tougher positions on their banks. For instance, when a severe drop in real estate prices in the late 1980s and early 1990s pushed Nordic banks into insolvency, their governments nationalized them. The United States, after initially failing to address its savings and loan problem in the 1980s, eventually closed insolvent institutions or sold them off to private buyers.

It is clear from these anecdotes that the Basel Accord serves at the convenience of its member countries.[31] To this day, members make their own decisions about enforcement, and no member country is penalized for failing to enforce the Accord's stated capital standards. Although it has perhaps contributed to greater consciousness of the useful role of regulatory capital among bankers and their observers in industry, media, and government, the Accord has proven toothless and, more important, has not achieved one of its fundamental goals: leveling the playing field in international banking.

Patching Up the Basel Accord

To its credit, the Basel committee admitted some of the standards' shortcomings and quickly went to work in the early 1990s to refine them.[32] However, much time passed before the committee could agree on any reforms. By 1996, when it did act, the committee made only one significant refinement to the initial standards: adding a separate capital calculation for short-term securities. This was not exactly the fundamental overhaul that was needed to address the fundamental problems just recited.

The Basel committee tried again in 1999, this time to address one of the Accord's main flaws: the arbitrariness of its four risk buckets. The proposal was to set risk weights for different types of loans by using ratings applied by private credit rating agencies. On the surface, this seemed like a positive step toward a market-based approach, but the committee's proposed overhaul quickly drew fire from all sides. Some critics argued that the rating agencies had a poor record of missing turning points and thus were not good indicators of risk. A related objection was that the ratings business, having only three or four major players in the United States, was not competitive. And in countries that had little or no experience with such agencies, the proposal was considered difficult, if not impossible, to implement.

So the committee went back to the drawing board and ultimately proposed two amendments to the original regime. The first was to add a new capital requirement for operating risks, such as interruption of the bank's computer network. The second was to allow the largest banks to use their own internal systems for evaluating loan riskiness, provided they could establish that they were sufficiently adept at evaluating and controlling risks. These changes and others became part of the so-called Basel II agreement, scheduled to be fully implemented in 2007.

The Basel process has dramatically demonstrated how a once simple set of standards can become highly complicated over time—the agreement is now more than 400 pages in length and riddled with mathematical formulae. But there is still no objective way to demonstrate whether the proposed new standards will be any more effective in discouraging imprudent risk taking. In fact, the opposite may be true.

Thus, one concern over the new Accord is that it might actually allow most large banks to hold *less capital* than they do now. This is because the revised rules, if adopted, will allow banks to use their own risk models to custom-tailor their capital requirements. The net result is that most large banks will have greater opportunities to take advantage of leverage and thus increase their returns on equity.[33] This outcome explains why many international banks support the new regime, despite its complexity. While it is conceivable that some of these banks have less risky portfolios and would thus require less capital, the disturbing possibility is that a number of other banks may take advantage of lower capital requirements to take greater risks. For a process that was launched, in part, to shore up banks against risk, this possibility is ironic. The irony thickens when we consider the fact that an international bank's failure would have the most serious impact on the international economy.

Even if large banks had to abide by Basel's risk standards, the standards are still so arbitrary that the regulated banks themselves can influence the process by which the standards are determined. A good example is Germany's persuading the committee to assign a 50 percent risk weight—half the weight for many other loans—to residential mortgages. There was no logic to the weighting except that German banks had heavy investments in real estate assets. The rest of the committee went along with this idea because other nations needed the Germans inside the system, especially given the high regard other central banks had for the German Bundesbank. Yet by bowing to the German demand, the committee dug a sizeable pit in the desired level playing field.

The integrity of the process is still not its greatest flaw, however. Its greatest flaw is that it is too cumbersome to keep pace with changes in financial technology and techniques. At their very best, domestic regulators are always one step behind the most sophisticated banks they regulate. The gap is bigger for international regulators. At the time of writing, it has been over five years since the latest changes were proposed to the Accord, and these will not even fully be implemented for another two. In an age marked by ever faster communications and a more rapid pace of change, a process like Basel grows ever more anachronistic.

Recognizing the shortcomings of the Basel capital rules, some countries have taken regulation into their own hands, thereby implicitly (if not explicitly) abandoning the quest for a level playing field. The United States, for example, has set up an extensive parallel system of capital regulation and enforcement. In 1989, Congress passed the Financial Institutions Reform, Recovery and Enforcement Act (FIRREA), which required thrift institutions (historically specializing in extending residential mortgages but since the early 1980s allowed to lend to consumers and businesses, like banks) to maintain minimum capital ratios of at least 3 percent. The ratios were calculated simply by dividing shareholders' equity by total assets and thus differed from the ratios under the Basel standards, where assets in different categories are given different weights and then added up.

In 1991, Congress enacted even tougher legislation for banks in the Federal Deposit Insurance Corporation Improvement Act (FDICIA). The act required regulators to set new, enforceable capital standards. More important, it put teeth into the requirements by establishing a new system of "prompt correction action" (PCA).[34] Under PCA, regulators had to impose progressively stiffer penalties the further a bank's capital went below the minimum requirement. Regulators were authorized to suspend banks' dividends, impose limits on its officers' salaries, and require that troubled banks issue more equity. Moreover, if a bank's capital fell below 2 percent of its assets—just short of insolvency—regulators could seize the bank and either close it down or, more likely, simply sell it.

The new regime worked. By the end of the decade, the average bank in the United States had a capital ratio in excess of 8 percent (unweighted), well above applicable regulatory minimums. Banks that had cavalierly skirted Basel's loopholes were suddenly carrying a safety margin of capital above the minimum to maintain a comfortable distance from the clutches of PCA.[35] High capital margins were further encouraged by new incentive schemes such as those embodied in the Gramm-Leach-Bliley Financial Modernization Act of 1999. That act permitted financial holding companies that own banks to own a range of other financial affiliates as well, provided their banks were well capitalized. Regulators have since decided that "well capitalized" means having a risk-weighted Tier 1 ratio of at least 6 percent of assets and a leverage ratio of capital to unweighted assets of at least 5 percent. Tellingly, the 6 percent ratio is actually higher than that required by Basel.

In short, the Basel Accord, with all its complex risk weightings and standards, has become almost irrelevant in the United States. Theoretically, it is more relevant in countries that have not adopted a set of parallel capital standards, but it is only as relevant as regulators decide to make it. Many countries have taken enforcement seriously and even adopted some version of PCA, based on the Basel formulae. Many have not and will continue to gamble on low capital ratios regardless of the Basel standards.

Fixing the Basel Accord the Right Way

Despite the Accord's serious flaws and de facto irrelevance, bank regulators in the member countries continue to worship at the altar of Basel. Banks also pay homage to the Accord, if for no other reason than not to offend their regulators. Too much time and political capital have been invested in the process of refining the Accord for the key players to abandon it.

Although the effort started with laudable objectives—to raise and internationalize bank capital standards—countries like the United States have found the unilateral route more effective. Nonetheless, there is a way to make the Accord truly effective, and to do so in a way that also comes close to the Accord's objective of leveling the playing field for banks from different countries. The simple solution is to mandate that all large banks back a fixed percentage of their assets with subordinated debt.[36]

Subordinated debt is what the term implies: long-term debt, i.e., bonds, held by creditors whose rights are subordinate to other secured creditors (those who have recourse to collateral if the borrower defaults) and depositors.[37] Holders of subordinated debt are entitled only to a fixed return and can redeem their bonds only after a clear maturity date. Furthermore, unlike deposits, this particular kind of debt is uninsured. In essence, if a bank fails, holders of subordinated debt get repaid after everyone else; which is to say, never.

Because they stand to lose the most from a bank failure, holders of subordinated debt have a vested interest in a bank's financial prudence. Even better, since their rate of return is fixed, they stand to gain nothing from a risky venture. These debt holders would therefore be an ideal check on a bank's more foolhardy tendencies. That check would function in two ways. The first way is through the market. The less stable a bank appears, the higher the interest rate bond buyers will demand. The higher the interest rate demanded by the buyers, the less subordinated debt a bank can sell. Since banks have to back a fixed percentage of their assets with subordinated debt, they can hold fewer assets if they sell less subordinated debt, so they cannot grow their business unless they prove to bond investors that their policies are sound. The second way the check would function is through better information gathering. Rising interest rates would serve as a clear warning signal to regulators that a bank is behaving badly. Given their incentives, holders of subordinated debt would be more motivated bank watchdogs than any government official. In order to make sure that those holders have the resources to serve their purpose reliably, regulators could require that subordinated debt be issued only in large denominations.[38]

Critics of a subordinated debt requirement argue that investors in such debt would provide no better signals of potential bank problems than bank regulators, who have access to nonpublic information about banks. This may or may not be true, but it is beside the point. Investors may be more accurate or less accurate, but investor incentives are clearly more powerful. As we have seen, regulators can all too easily exercise forbearance and allow troubled banks to gamble for resurrection, especially if the government demands it. Investors, on the other hand, put their precious capital at risk by looking the other way. Forbearance is not an option in the subordinated debt market. Subordinated debt holders would never have encouraged the banks to lend so irresponsibly in the 1970s.

Trade and Investment Politics

Though the Basel process was at times influenced by the banks it purported to regulate, their influence should have been an exception to the rule—international standards were supposed to shape banks' policies, not the other way around. However, the exception may have indeed become the rule. This is increasingly apparent in the sphere of foreign trade and investment policy, where a broad range of financial institutions have become increasingly important players. Bankers around the world have begun to see trade and investment policy as the key to entering foreign markets.

Trade policy, the precursor to cross-border investment policy, is carried out with sticks and carrots, or combinations of both. The sticks are sanctions, which governments at various points have imposed on exports to some countries or on imports from others in efforts to persuade them to behave differently. Sanctions can be an effective tool of foreign policy, but only if they are imposed multilaterally, so that the target country cannot get supplies or funds from other sources. The most recent comprehensive study of this subject concluded that 34 percent of multilateral economic sanctions were successful in achieving their stated foreign policy aims, while unilateral sanctions had only an 18 percent success rate.[39] As policy tools, therefore, the effectiveness of sanctions is limited by the amount of international support they receive.

More typically, trade policy is carried out with carrots offered in trade negotiations that are analogous to arms reduction talks. The carrots are the concessions countries are willing to make to open their markets if other countries take similar measures. Tariffs are thus treated like ballistic missiles—they are only taken down when others reciprocate. Since the end of World War II, the General Agreement on Tariffs and Trade

(GATT)—now the World Trade Organization (WTO)—has provided the forum for gradually reducing trade barriers around the world. After eight successive rounds of multilateral trade negotiations, for example, tariffs have been cut from an average of 40 percent to just 6 percent (although many developing countries still maintain much higher tariffs on selected products).[40]

Until the Uruguay Round of world trade talks, completed in 1994, governments concentrated their attention on trade in goods. But while goods still account for most international trade overall, they make up less than half the output of rich countries. Trade in services—including financial services—has become increasingly important. For example, though the United States ran an overall trade deficit of more than $400 billion in 2003, it had a surplus of $66 billion in services trade. However, barriers to trade in services still exist in many forms. Among the most important are rules or practices that inhibit the ability of foreign companies to establish themselves in other countries. In effect, because they cannot invest in these countries by establishing themselves there, these companies cannot trade their services. That is why the first General Agreement on Trade in Services (GATS), negotiated during the Uruguay Round and initiated in January 1995, clearly affirmed for services firms the right of establishment, defined as the right of a foreign company to set up a business in a way no different from that required of domestic firms.

Financial services firms in rich countries were especially active in urging their governments to conclude the GATS, whose initial provisions became effective in 1999. But securing the right of establishment was only a first step. Many countries still maintain screening boards that decide not only whether a foreign financial institution is fit to do business in a country, but whether the institution is needed. The latter condition is not consistent with open markets, since it acts as an invitation to exclude entry altogether. Other restrictions include those on the corporate form in which foreign firms can do business; requirements that foreign firms form joint ventures with local partners (who in many cases must have majority control); and restrictions on doing business from other countries via the Internet or other means of cross-border communication. In short, financial services firms are still not given national treatment—the same treatment given domestic firms—when doing business in many countries.

Understandably, U.S. financial services firms have been pressing U.S. trade negotiators to insert national treatment clauses into the various bilateral agreements they negotiate, as well as into the current WTO Doha Round of world trade talks.[41] But these firms are not content with gaining national treatment in law and in fact.[42] They have pressed U.S. negotiators in the context of recent bilateral free trade agreement negotiations (such as the one with Singapore) to ensure that other countries remove all of their controls on the movement of capital into and out of those countries. This position is not hard to understand. Financial services firms are essentially in the business of moving money, and any governmental restrictions on that process impede their ability to do business. Many economists side with them, arguing that controls on the movement of capital are no different from restrictions on trade: both interfere with the freedom of contract, and both make commerce less efficient.

While capital controls have many drawbacks, their opponents should draw an important lesson from the Asian financial crisis: capital controls are *not* the equivalent of trade restrictions, especially for developing countries. Capital controls have been put in place generally because governments fear that their citizens and foreign investors, in a panic, can drive down the value of their currencies. This can be economically destabilizing when domestic firms that have borrowed in dollars, as many Asian firms did prior to the crisis, suddenly have to scramble for much more domestic currency than they thought would be required to pay off their dollar-denominated debts. As we discuss at length in chapter 6, this problem is simply endemic to a world in which national monies are mandated by governments yet unwanted by those who must use them. This is why countries that controlled capital outflows, such as India and China, were hardly touched by the Asian crisis.

Our point is *not* that capital controls are good—rationing access to capital necessarily raises its cost, and efforts to circumvent or manipulate restrictions are, at best, distortionary and wasteful. Our point is that there is a more sensible path to opening up capital markets that would avoid the kind of turmoil unleashed in 1998: "dollarization." This is a broad term we apply to any policy that abandons unstable local monies in favor of the dollar, euro, or some other internationally accepted money. But that idea, discussed more fully in chapter 6, is one for the longer term. In the here and now, policymakers and trade negotiators should simply act with greater prudence, not with misplaced free-market dogmatism, when dealing with capital controls. After all, there is nothing free market about government-produced monopoly monies (pun intended) in the first place.

Trade and investment policy is an area in which what may be good for certain financial institutions in the United States and elsewhere in the rich world may not be good for the economic health of developing countries with weak monetary systems and underdeveloped, poorly regulated banking and financial systems. Ultimately, it may not even be in the wider interests of the United States, for, as we shall see in chapter 5, financial crises abroad create security as well as economic risks at home. As the world's financial system becomes ever more integrated globally, so grows the need for better international regulatory coordination to reduce the risks of weaknesses in one country spreading problems to others. But the lessons of the Basel process's failings need to be heeded on many levels, as we will see in our analysis of financial crises in chapter 6: problems of institutional weakness, poor incentives, and inadequate monitoring are most effectively addressed by harnessing the natural driving forces of the market itself.

3

FINANCE AND THE "WAR ON TERROR"

Only days after the terrorist attacks of September 11, 2001, President George W. Bush announced a far-reaching "war on terror." He not only signed legislation to strengthen law enforcement tools against actual and would-be terrorists, but also embraced the Clinton administration's campaign to dry up the financial flows to terrorists. The latter step was a striking about-face. Only months before, two top economic officials, then-Treasury Secretary Paul O'Neill and chief economic adviser Lawrence Lindsey, had questioned the wisdom of the Clinton administration's anti–money laundering effort.[1]

That governments can fight the post-9/11 war on terror by stopping the flow of money to terrorists seems like a reasonable proposition on its face. After all, if it were possible to deny terrorists access to sources of finance—and specifically access to financial institutions—then it might be possible either to keep them from engaging in their nefarious activities, or at least to raise the cost of such activities significantly and thereby interrupt some of them. But even if the efforts to track and seize the finances of terrorists failed to impede them, mounting a financial war on terrorists might help law enforcement officials and the military locate, apprehend, or even kill them before they strike again.

How might such a war be carried out? Governments can stop the terrorist money flow at its source or in its transmission. An example of a source-based policy is the crackdown by U.S. and other national authorities on supposed charities that, in fact, are terrorist fronts. Shut them down, or seize their money, or both. This is straightforward law enforcement; it is important, but it is not our focus in this chapter.

What interests us instead is how the United States and other governments have enlisted financial institutions in the war on terror by imposing various requirements on them aimed at exposing and interrupting the transmission of money raised in one place to support terrorist activities somewhere else. The name for this transmission process is money laundering. Narrowly defined, money laundering is the "conversion of criminal incomes into assets that cannot be traced back to the underlying crime."[2] In the United States, the term historically has been associated with organized crime and drug trafficking. In a post-9/11 world, money laundering has become a principal means by which terrorism is financed.

Money is best laundered at the most efficient financial laundries: banks. The terrorists who carried out the 9/11 attacks and their financiers used banks as intermediaries in the same way everyone else does. Depositors put their money in an institution in one place and then instruct the institution to pay someone who has a bank account somewhere else. If they can get away with it, terrorists can and will use financial institutions in exactly the same way. The problem comes when they use the money to finance acts of terror.

The U.S. government—and other governments—have used and strengthened anti–money laundering (AML) laws to keep terrorists from using regulated financial institutions. The campaign has not been as effective as it could be. Fortunately, there are ways to do it better.

Anti–Money Laundering, Drugs, and the Roots of the Financial War on Terror

Many of the regulations used in the financial war on terror have their origins in the war against illegal drugs. Like terrorists, drug traffickers use or try to use financial institutions to carry out their activities. Drugs flow all too easily across national borders; money even more so. That is why the United States has tried to enlist other countries in its AML efforts. The target has not been small. In 1998, then-director of the International Monetary Fund Michel Camdessus estimated that $800 billion to $2 trillion was laundered worldwide each year, equivalent to about 2–5 percent of worldwide gross domestic product.[3]

The AML regime has developed gradually. In broad outlines, it has had three features: the reporting of currency transactions to enable governmental agencies to better detect, track, and apprehend suspected criminals; requirements that financial institutions know their customers and screen out undesirables; and rules that institutions check their customer information against government-compiled lists of suspicious individuals and organizations.

Reporting

The U.S. government began its AML campaign by asking depository institutions—banks and "savings and loans"—to help detect drug trafficking and other criminal activity. The Bank Secrecy Act of 1970 (BSA) required these depositories to report certain transactions to the Treasury Department. The reports covered cash deposits and withdrawals, importations of currency of $10,000 or more, so-called suspicious transactions involving more than $5,000, cross-border currency transactions, and information relating to foreign bank and securities accounts. Regulators enforce these requirements through administrative sanctions and, potentially, civil and criminal penalties. The Patriot Act of 2001 extended the reach of the BSA reporting requirements beyond depositories to other financial institutions (see below).

The BSA provisions were designed to deter drug lords and other criminals from using U.S. depository institutions to help fund their unlawful activities. The requirements also provided law enforcement officials with information to target their investigations and apprehend criminals.

Drug traffickers nonetheless quickly found their way around the reporting regime. To get around the $10,000 threshold, they simply broke up their cash deposits and withdrawals into smaller amounts, a process that came to be called smurfing. They also used the proceeds of their drugs-related activities to finance otherwise legitimate businesses—restaurants, laundries, and the like. Criminals would mix their ill-gotten gains with the monies taken in by these establishments and thereby launder the proceeds from drug trafficking.

In 1982, the Treasury Department tried to counter this activity by requiring U.S. financial institutions to file suspicious activity reports (SARs). These are reports on individual financial transactions that should, at least in principle, call attention to possible drug trafficking, money laundering, or other financially related crimes (such as wire fraud). The U.S. government now coordinates its investigations of suspected drug traffickers through a nine-agency task force chaired by the Justice Department.[4]

Know Your Customers

Sixteen years after passage of the BSA, Congress imposed additional requirements on financial institutions. This time the effort sought to enlist the institutions in watching out for suspected criminal activity and, ideally, refusing to accept suspicious accounts. The statutory vehicle was the Money Laundering Control Act of 1986 (MLCA). That act required U.S. financial institutions to know their customers by exercising due diligence on potential new accounts. Institutions would have to require proof of identity (name, address, Social Security number, credit references, and the like) and employment history. The act was initially aimed at drug traffickers, but over time lawmakers have added other offenses to the act.[5] After 9/11, Congress tightened these minimal requirements through the Patriot Act, which we discuss shortly.[6]

List Checking

The U.S. government not only requires financial institutions to watch out for suspicious activity, but in addition does so itself. Then, at least in principle, it shares the information it uncovers with private institutions so they can better stop illicit activity at its inception. For instance, the Office of Foreign Asset Control (OFAC) in the Treasury maintains a constantly updated list of undesirable individuals and organizations with whom financial institutions are not supposed to do business. Other federal agencies keep similar lists. Roughly a year after 9/11 the president ordered the agencies to merge their data into a single master list, which was to become operational by the end of 2003. Yet, according to the General Accounting Office, as of mid-2004 the federal government had still not produced such a list, and critics say it may take years to do so.[7]

Well before September 11, the Treasury Department took its own steps to integrate AML enforcement measures. In 1990, the department established the Financial Crimes Enforcement Network (FINCEN). FINCEN now shares information provided by banks and other financial institutions covered by the BSA with local, state, and federal law enforcement agencies. FINCEN also provides support for the investigation of individual money laundering cases and attempts to identify financial crime patterns from the financial information it receives. The network operates internationally as well, sharing similar information with foreign enforcement officials.

Meanwhile, banks have purchased commercially developed software to help them check current and potential customers against the OFAC list and possibly other lists, though even the best programs still generate some false positives; that is, individuals who appear to match the list but in fact are not criminals or terrorists. Banks aim to have a false positive target rate on the order of 1 percent or less, although experts differ as to whether such a low rate is feasible.

International Cooperation on Money Laundering

Money laundering and the crimes related to it cannot be fought effectively by U.S. law enforcement officials alone. Money flows across national borders too easily for any one country to staunch the flow of resources to criminals and terrorists. U.S. policymakers have therefore made efforts for over a decade to enlist the aid of other countries. In 1989, the United States and France persuaded other members of the Group of 7 (G-7) to form a Financial Action Task Force (FATF), primarily to thwart drug trafficking through financial regulation. Since then, the FATF has grown to a total of 33 member countries. It has set standards for country-led efforts to combat money laundering. More important, it has authorized member states to "name and shame" nations that have inadequate laws and enforcement by blocking their access to the markets of FATF states.

The naming and shaming system appears to have worked reasonably well. In 2000, the FATF placed 15 countries on the list. Eight others have been added since, but as of year-end 2004, a total of 19 had been removed because they upgraded their vigilance against money laundering and persuaded the task force of that fact. Of particular significance, both Switzerland and the Cayman Islands, long havens for laundered money, have responded in recent years to strong international pressure to relax their once strict bank secrecy laws and to cooperate with foreign law enforcement officials.

Two reasons explain the success of the name and shame regime. First, financially powerful FATF member states have agreed to impose sanctions multilaterally.[8] Second, access to these countries' financial institutions and markets is important for countries that have sought to remove themselves from the lists. Still, even with 33 countries in the FTAF banding together to deny access to their markets, four countries remained on the name and shame list at the close of 2004.[9]

In 1990, the FATF also issued a widely publicized list of "40 Recommendations" to combat money laundering. These recommendations consisted of standards for financial supervision and criminal law enforcement.[10] By 1996, more than 130 countries had endorsed the recommendations. But while the FATF has sponsored peer reviews of countries to determine to what extent they comply with these standards, the task force has no independent authority to sanction countries for failing to live up to them, other than to name and shame them. Of equal or greater importance, the FATF standards refer only to statutes or regulations on the books, not to how effectively they are enforced.

The Post-9/11 Financial War on Terrorism

The AML campaign expanded into the war on terror even before the terrorist attacks of September 11. During his two terms in office, President Clinton froze the U.S. assets of various alleged state sponsors of terrorism, including Iraq, Libya, Syria, and the Taliban regime in Afghanistan. In 1995, Clinton added 12 Middle Eastern groups as terrorist organizations and ordered their assets to be frozen. The same executive order directed the Treasury Department to freeze assets of designated individual terrorists. In 1996, the Omnibus Antiterrorism Act extended the asset freeze authority to every group that the secretary of state had designated a Foreign Terrorist Organization.[11] Meanwhile, the Clinton administration pushed the FATF to name and shame numerous countries that failed to adopt and implement an adequate AML control regime (for example, one including "know your customer" and asset freeze policies).

As we noted at the outset, the Bush administration came into office questioning the value of this effort. Then came September 11. The attacks brought a new sense of urgency to combating terrorism in all possible ways, including measures aimed at drying up financial sources for terrorism. After all, the administration could not afford to be seen as allowing terrorists unrestricted access to legitimate financial institutions. In addition, administration officials hoped that a reinvigorated AML effort might at least provide leads to help locate, apprehend, or kill terrorists after the fact, even if it failed in preventing them from carrying out their acts.

The USA Patriot Act of 2001

The new AML effort focused much more heavily on regulation than on seizure of assets. At the end of 1999, just before President Bush assumed office, roughly $3 billion in assets had already been frozen, almost all from designated state sponsors of terrorism. (Iraq accounted for $1.5 billion and Libya just under $1 billion.)[12] By the end of 2002, over a year after the terrorist attacks on September 11, 2001, that amount had risen only modestly, to $4 billion.[13]

The regulatory campaign, in contrast, was extensive, as illustrated by the following provisions in the USA Patriot Act:

> • The act extended the reporting of cash transactions above $10,000 beyond banks and securities brokers to casinos, car dealers, and a range of other U.S. firms. In related fashion, the act extended SAR filing requirements to securities brokers and dealers, commodity merchants, and advisers. Together, these measures were designed to make it easier for law enforcement officials to identify and apprehend terrorists before they act.
> • The act supplemented existing "know your customer" rules with new requirements for collecting and screening customers wanting to open new accounts. Financial institutions would have to verify customers not only by examining their documents, but

also by visiting their premises and conducting Internet searches. These requirements, too, were designed to keep terrorists and their supporters from using any legitimate U.S. financial institutions.

• The act enabled the executive branch to restrict or prohibit access to the U.S. financial system by states and foreign financial institutions that have inadequate AML controls.

• The act demanded that all U.S. financial institutions have policies, procedures, and controls in place to identify instances in which their correspondent and private banking accounts with foreign individuals and organizations might be used for money laundering. A correspondent account is defined by the Patriot Act as one that is established by a U.S.-based institution for a foreign bank to allow the latter to do business in the United States without maintaining a physical presence there.

• The act gave the attorney general and the Treasury Department unprecedented authority to demand information from U.S. financial institutions about their foreign-held correspondent accounts, while requiring U.S. institutions to comply with enhanced due diligence standards to assure that their correspondent banks are not laundering money. Though regulators since have provided little guidance about exactly how U.S. institutions are to meet these standards, the Federal Reserve settled a case in July 2004 with ABN AMRO Bank (a major Dutch bank) and its New York branch requiring this institution to be more vigilant in conducting business with correspondent banks. The motivation behind this enforcement action, and more broadly the legislation that authorized it, is to prevent foreign banks from using the U.S. financial system to launder money from abroad.

International Cooperation

The 2001 attacks on the World Trade Center were funded by a network of business enterprises, bank accounts, and NGOs around the world.[14] Preventing future attacks will require an effort that covers the same amount of territory; in short, the effort must be truly international. To its credit, the Bush administration has recognized this and has continued to have its officials participate in various forums that were established under prior administrations to exchange views and information about how best to use financial regulation to inhibit terrorism. The forums include the United Nations Counter-Terrorism Committee, the International Monetary Fund (IMF), the World Bank, and, perhaps most important, the FATF.[15] Indeed, after 9/11, the FATF supplemented its previous 40 recommendations aimed at money laundering with eight additional standards or recommendations for combating terrorist financing in particular. By at least one account, these multilateral initiatives have induced a number of countries—notably, Bahrain, Lebanon, the United Arab Emirates, and Egypt—to toughen their AML regimes.[16]

These forums are not equally effective, however. While the IMF, for example, has expanded its role in the financial war on terror as part of its Financial Sector Assessment Program (FSAP), the results of this expansion are uncertain. Introduced in 1999, the FSAPs assess the adequacy of financial supervision and legal infrastructure in IMF member countries. In a very general way, that infrastructure includes regulation to prevent financial crime and money laundering. In reality, however, we know of no instance in which the IMF has denied lending to a country because it failed adequately to police these acts. The IMF also provides technical advice on stopping money laundering and methods for improving "know your customer" procedures. But advice is useless unless governments have the will and resources to follow it. In any event, participation by member countries in the FSAP process is voluntary, which should further illustrate how limited the IMF role is in the overall AML regime.

Limitations of the Financial War on Terror

However far-reaching the new financial regulations may appear on paper, their effectiveness in curbing terrorism is severely limited by three major factors. The first is America's capacity to implement the new regulations. In the private sector, some 3,200 banks, 6,000 brokerage firms, and 4,400 insurance companies have yet to implement basic watch lists to screen new customers.[17] Even so, banks have actually expanded their annual reporting from 100,000 SARs between 1998 and 2000 to roughly 300,000 between 2003 and 2004.[18] This might seem encouraging but for the fact that the Treasury Department does not have the personnel to follow up on most of these reports.[19] In fact, the General Accounting Office concluded in September 2003 that severe underfunding of the Patriot Act, coupled with a lack of cooperation between law enforcement officials and regulators, was undermining the financial regulatory provisions of the act.[20]

Other countries are even more lacking in funds and personnel. While OFAC has over a hundred staff working full-time on implementation of financial sanctions (and, as we saw, is still unable to keep up with the level of reporting), the counterpart agency in Great Britain has only about seven staff members, the one in France two, and the one in Germany just one.[21] Some of America's European allies, for their part, complain that U.S. law enforcement officials do not fully share intelligence on many suspected terrorists. This makes it impossible for other countries to block their accounts or seize their assets.

Even if the regulatory system had everything it needed, its effectiveness in fighting terror would still be limited by a second factor: underground financial networks. Many means of holding and transporting money are not part of the official world financial system and are not subject to its regulations. Since the U.S. military and law enforcement crackdown, the terrorist organization Al Qaeda reportedly has resorted to old-fashioned couriers who carry hundreds of thousands of dollars with them. They also use the ancient *hawala* banking system, through which individuals (primarily in the Middle East and South Asia) transfer money without leaving a paper trail. This occurs when a customer in one location deposits funds with a trusted *hawaladar*, who asks another trusted counterparty to distribute money out of his own funds to the intended beneficiary. Because the hawaladars trust each other, and indeed often come from the same family, they expect to be paid back from transactions going the other way. Ultimately, if they have to, they can settle their debts some time in the future. Confidence in the entire system is based on this built-up trust. Hawala is legal in most countries in which it takes place (though not in India), but it is unregulated and therefore very difficult to monitor, especially because there is no paper trail for investigators to uncover.

Authorities in the United States and the FATF member countries have made some effort to bring the hawala system into the sunlight. But there are inherent limits to the effectiveness of this campaign. Even if government officials could enforce the registration of all hawala brokers, and even if those brokers left paper or electronic markings that could be tracked, it is highly unlikely that officials could successfully distinguish between funds legitimately transferred by the millions of individuals in the developing world and immigrants in developed countries for legitimate purposes and the illegitimate transfers that further terrorism.

All of these efforts at regulation are limited even further by a third factor: acts of terror are cheap to carry out. The truck bomb used at the World Trade Center in February 1993 cost $400.[22] The cost of training and support of the 19 individuals who participated in the 9/11 airline hijackings is estimated at only $500,000.[23] Terrorist operations since 9/11 have been even cheaper: the October 2002 Indonesia bombings cost $50,000; the November 2003 Istanbul attacks cost less than $40,000; and the March 2004 Madrid bombings, carried out with dynamite and cell phones, cost less than $10,000.[24] As Defense Secretary Donald Rumsfeld admitted in a memorandum leaked to the press in October 2003, "The cost-benefit ratio is against us! Our cost is billions against the terrorist cost of millions."[25]

These limitations cast doubt on the effectiveness of the financial war on terror. Some policymakers have recognized this. While the *9/11 Commission Report,* for instance, asserts that efforts to track terrorist financing should remain "front and center in U.S. counterterrorism efforts," it also acknowledges that asset freezing will diminish in effectiveness as terrorists find more ways to go around the system.[26] As we have seen, the same can be said for AML regulation. In light of these doubts, we need to take a more rigorous look at the costs and benefits of the AML campaign.

High Costs, Elusive Benefits

We have seen the limitations of the financial war on terror, but it is important to consider as rigorously as possible whether the benefits of the campaign have been worth the costs. After all, precisely this type of calculus must be made in other spheres of regulatory activity. There is no reason for making an exception when it comes to a financial war on terror, however important some may deem it to be. Unfortunately, the quantitative assessment of this effort is hindered by considerable limitations of its own. The costs, when quantifiable, are often scattered and hidden in myriad budget lines. The benefits, when measurable, cannot be definitively attributed to AML regulation in particular.

While we are still at an early stage in the implementation of the AML measures required by the Patriot Act, a number of studies have been done on the actual and predicted costs of compliance with the AML regime. Following Peter Reuter and Ted Truman, who have conducted the most thorough analysis of the costs of the AML regime, we will separate the costs into three categories: those incurred by the government in administering the AML laws and regulations; those incurred by the private sector to comply with the regime; and other costs borne by the public.[27]

The costs incurred by the government can be estimated from numbers in an account in the U.S. budget called the "750 account," which covers the administration of justice generally. Reuter and Truman have adjusted the figures from this account to arrive at their best judgment that the U.S. government's AML spending is on the order of $1.5 billion annually. When state and local expenditures are added, the total estimated public sector expense is $3 billion.[28]

The additional costs borne by financial institutions are also significant. A recent survey of banks worldwide has found that the average cost of AML compliance has risen 61 percent between 2001 and 2004, and it is expected to rise further.[29] In fact, 29 percent of respondents to the survey in North America have more than doubled their spending, the largest factors in that increase being transaction monitoring, training, and reporting to regulators. A 2003 study estimated that in the mutual fund industry alone compliance with the Customer Identification Program would cost $288 million in the first year of implementation and $140 million annually thereafter. This comes to approximately $13 per "new relationship."[30] But this is still only a small fraction of the total private sector cost. Using estimates of several private consulting firms, Reuter and Truman suggest that this figure is in the range of $3 billion per year.[31]

As for direct costs to the general public, Reuter and Truman estimate these at roughly an additional $1 billion.[32] However, these costs do not include the nonquantifiable costs of intrusions into the privacy of law-abiding individuals whose accounts may be scrutinized as part of the AML dragnet. Nor do they include any consumer inconvenience resulting from questions and inquiries required as part of the "know your customer" rules.

In total, Reuter and Truman estimate the cost of the AML regime at approximately $7 billion per year. This cost likely grew in 2004 as regulators have become more aggressive in the regime's enforcement.[33] But can we say that these costs have had corresponding benefits? Not with any certainty. In principle, the benefits would take two forms: reductions in terrorism and assistance to law enforcement and the military in the apprehension of terrorists. In practice, however, it is essentially impossible for anyone outside the government to get an even rough estimate of these benefits.

The extent of the rise or decline in terrorism is a quantity that even those inside the government have had difficulty estimating. For instance, while the State Department's 2003 terrorism report claimed to show a decline in terrorist activity, it had to be disavowed because of "methodological flaws."[34] Secretary Rumsfeld, in a remarkable moment of candor, admitted in a memorandum leaked to the press in October 2003, "Today, we lack metrics to know if we are winning or losing the global war on terror."

Even if we did have such metrics, we still could not legitimately infer whether and to what extent the AML regime has hampered or deterred terrorists. Even if the State Department report had been right about the decline in terrorism, for instance, there would still be no hard basis upon which to ascribe any such success to tighter financial regulation.

Measuring the contribution of AML regulation to law enforcement is also problematic. The role of regulation in helping officials to locate, halt, or apprehend specific terrorists cannot be verified by anyone outside the government. While there is some anecdotal evidence that, in particular cases, SARs have led officials to find criminals who have been subsequently convicted, the connection between this evidence and the war on terror is virtually undetectable.[35]

The upshot of this assessment is that America is spending at least $7 billion a year on unproven initiatives to fight a financial war on terror.

To put this finding in some meaningful perspective, there is a host of compelling homeland security initiatives that are in dire need of that kind of money. For instance, we currently have no effective system for monitoring and verifying the contents of the world's 90 million container shipments per year.[36] As a result, any one of those containers could contain an explosive, possibly nuclear, device. If loaded onto one of the 8 million containers that pass through U.S. ports each year, the device's detonation could shut down all shipments into and out of the United States for several weeks or even months, thereby causing an economic disaster.[37] What would it cost to implement an effective worldwide container security system? Stephen Flynn, a leading expert on homeland security, estimates it would cost roughly $40 to $80 per shipment, or $4 to $7 billion per year.[38] In other words, for the same amount of money that is spent domestically on possibly fruitless AML initiatives, we could institute a global security system that would significantly reduce the risk of a crippling shutdown of the international commercial network.

In light of the clear opportunity costs of America's spending on antiterrorism financial regulation, we must ask whether we have fully encompassed the reasons for it in our discussion. The answer may be that we have left out an important public diplomacy dimension to such spending. As the terrorism expert Paul Pillar suggests, by mounting a financial war on terrorism the United States signals to other countries the seriousness with which it takes the terrorist threat, and may thereby be able to influence other governments to take the matter seriously as well.[39] A government that condemns terrorism and demands that other countries make political and financial sacrifices in order to stop it cannot afford to appear to be allowing its financial institutions to abet terrorist financing with impunity. Seen in this light, the financial war on terror is a necessary component of a wider initiative to draw nations with disparate interests into visible cooperation against a threat which is widely felt but often difficult to combat, for political reasons, through more aggressive means.

Going Forward

The public diplomacy element of the financial war on terror is important enough that the campaign will continue, notwithstanding significant hard-dollar opportunity costs. It can, however, be made a more efficient and effective component of a comprehensive political and military approach to deterring, detecting, and responding to terrorism. Here is what should be done in the United States and wider afield.

Within the United States, the first vital step toward waging a smarter campaign is to improve coordination among the different arms of the AML regime. It is imperative that the president assign top priority to coordinating all of the agencies that now have their own lists of suspicious individuals and organizations—the Departments of Homeland Security, Defense, Justice, Treasury, among others—to develop and regularly maintain a master list of all such individuals and organizations. Such a list would greatly assist each of the agencies involved in carrying out its own specific functions related to locating, apprehending, and deterring terrorists.

Once this list is created, financial institutions should have access to it. As a fallback, even if a consolidated list were not created (or effectively maintained), the president should direct each of the federal agencies that now have their own lists to share them on a regular basis with authorized individuals in private financial institutions. Although the Patriot Act envisioned a two-way street between the public and private spheres, the information flow has been almost entirely one way thus far. With the exception of the Treasury Department, government agencies have provided little or no information to the financial institutions charged by the government with watching out for terrorists. In turn, financial institutions, with little or no government information on which to base their reporting standards, have covered themselves legally by inundating these agencies with SARs and Currency Transaction Reports (CTRs) related to activities that look even remotely suspicious. An accessible master list of suspicious persons and groups, or at least regular reporting of such information by each of the agencies to the financial institutions, would provide the institutions with a more effective way of focusing their screening on the greatest risks. Ultimately, this would save time and money both for the financial institutions and the government, and transform a costly paper-passing exercise into one that is far more likely to assist authorities in identifying transactions tied to terrorist and other illegal activities.

Government agencies may resist a shift toward more information sharing because they fear security leaks. In particular, if those individuals on the list knew of that fact, they and their colleagues might be able to infer the sources and the methods used to identify them. This could compromise the efforts of law enforcement and intelligence agencies to gain useful information about terrorists and their organizations in the future. But security has long been an issue for defense contractors, and it is addressed by requiring private sector individuals who work with the government on sensitive matters to get security clearances equivalent to those who work for the government itself. The same process can and should be applied to individuals in financial institutions who obtain sensitive information about potential or actual terrorists (or criminals).

These efforts will help streamline efforts to combat terrorist financing without imposing further costs on financial intermediation that would ultimately be borne by savers and companies seeking to raise capital. Their ultimate effectiveness, however, hinges on whether other countries implement equally effective measures. As we emphasized earlier and will demonstrate again in chapter 4, any form of financial monitoring or sanction scheme simply must be multilateral as long as the target can move funds to, or raise funds in, alternative legal jurisdictions.

The best way to proceed is to build on past successes. As we discussed, the FATF has been successful in getting numerous countries to tighten their AML regulations. Its scope must now be expanded in order to ensure that countries actually implement and enforce the laws on their books.

The FATF will need modestly increased resources to evaluate and monitor AML enforcement—using metrics such as amount of money and number of individuals dedicated to enforcement—in different countries. If a country suspected of failing to carry out enforcement commitments could not adequately document its efforts to the task force or demonstrate them on-site, it would be subject to name and shame sanctions—a response that has already demonstrated its effectiveness in improving cooperation and motivating compliance.

Of course, it would be unfair and pointless to sanction a country that does not have the funds to execute its laws in the first place. Therefore, the United States and other wealthy member states should offer aid packages to finance enforcement measures in other countries. The United States already provides roughly $1 billion annually across 67 developing countries to help them stem the supply of illegal drugs.[40] A comparable sum provided in total by the richer members of the FATF would go a long way toward securing effective global cooperation and increased effectiveness in the AML effort.

4

CAPITAL MARKETS SANCTIONS

This is going to be the sanctions wave of the future.
—Anonymous U.S. congressional aide

Of Markets and Metaphors

Approach a medieval European city, and the importance of religious authority is immediately apparent in the cathedral dominating the skyline. In a seventeenth-century city, it is the secular authority that is elevated, literally and metaphorically, through the towering presence of the political palace. In a modern city, it is the power of the commercial sector, and particularly its financial institutions, that is reflected in the gleaming skyscrapers.[1]

Buildings are metaphors for emergent centers of power. Politics provides such metaphors as well. In international affairs, the granting or withholding of trade "privileges" has taken on great symbolic meaning since the end of the Cold War. America, as the national embodiment of the emergent global power of international commerce and finance, bestows free-trade agreements on nations that aid her in the war on terrorism. (Pakistan was so blessed by the Bush administration in 2001, even though Congress declined to convert the metaphor into actual commerce.)[2] America also punishes with economic sanctions those who oppose her. For those large enough to be particularly irksome in their opposition, such as China and Russia, the ultimate surrogate for traditional warfare has become capital markets sanctions. How did capital markets assume center stage in the emerging drama of financial statecraft?

Congress Targets Homeland Securities

The idea of restricting access to the U.S. capital markets in the service of foreign policy aims was thrust into the political arena by three prominent congressionally mandated reports published between 1999 and 2002, and focused largely on security issues related to China. By 2001, the idea had already been fashioned into a sanctions provision contained in draft legislation aimed at deterring foreign companies from doing business in Sudan. We discuss these initiatives below.

The Cox Committee and Deutch Commission Reports

In 1999, two bodies created by Congress released reports related to activities of the Chinese military and their links to Chinese commercial and financial activities either in the United States or involving U.S. firms. The conclusions of the reports were headline-grabbing in their focus on the purported role of the U.S. capital markets in providing finance, however indirectly, for Chinese weapons development and proliferation.

The first of these reports was prepared by the Cox Committee, named for its chairman, Representative Christopher Cox (R-CA). The committee was established in 1998 to investigate concerns over Chinese acquisition of sensitive U.S. missile and space technology.[3] Its remit was subsequently expanded to cover alleged security problems and possible espionage at U.S. nuclear weapons laboratories. The report's conclusions present a sensational picture of a Chinese government determined to acquire sensitive American military technology through the use of a vast network of spies, visiting researchers, and front companies operating in the United States.

The report asserted tantalizingly that there were "more than 3,000 PRC corporations in the United States, *some* with links to the PLA, a State intelligence service, or with technology targeting and acquisition roles" (emphasis added).[4] The report never indicates how many "some" might be.

"The idea that most of these companies are set up by the [state security agency] is absolute nonsense," according to the China economy expert Nicholas Lardy.[5] The State Department had in 1997 identified two PLA companies operating in the United States, and James Mulvenon, a specialist on the Chinese military's commercial activities who testified before the Cox Committee, put the number of PLA-affiliated companies at between 20 and 30.[6] So where did the number 3,000 come from?

Cox himself said later that he used the number merely "to suggest the possible scope of the problem." Comparable "suggestions" in the report's political, economic, scientific, and military analysis led an interdisciplinary assessment of the report, conducted through Stanford University's Center for International Security and Cooperation, to conclude that its "discussion of Chinese politics, economic modernization, and nuclear doctrine lacks scholarly rigor, and exhibits too many examples of sloppy research, factual errors, and weakly justified inferences."[7]

The second report, released in July 1999, was prepared by the Deutch Commission,[8] named for its chairman, former CIA Director John Deutch, which was established in 1996 to investigate proliferation of weapons of mass destruction (WMD). The Deutch Commission report focused heavily on the final conclusion of the Cox Committee report that China "is using U.S. capital markets both as a source of central government funding for military and commercial development and as a means of cloaking U.S. technology acquisition efforts by its front companies with a patina of regularity and respectability," and that the Securities and Exchange Commission (SEC) failed to collect enough information to allow effective monitoring of Chinese commercial activities in the United States. The Deutch Commission concluded that

> because there is currently no national security-based review of entities seeking to gain access to our capital markets, investors are unlikely to know that they may be assisting in the proliferation of weapons of mass destruction by providing funds to known proliferators. Aside from the moral implications, there are potential financial consequences of proliferation activity—such as the imposition of trade and financial sanctions—which could negatively impact investors.

This last sentence has proven a rallying cry not only for anti-China and national security hawks, but for activists of all stripes. A new logic had been proffered in a major, congressionally mandated report that could be used to compel the U.S. government to harness the power of the capital markets, despised by groups on the right and left of the political spectrum, in the service of any manner of Great Cause. The logic was that since foreign companies doing wrong might be hit by American government punishment in consequence, American investors in such companies must receive government warnings of such companies' behavior, presumably in a manner such that they would be deterred from investing.

Tellingly, however, the logic was not deemed two-sided or universal. That is, first, activities designated as being bad by activists could only be assumed to be bad for investors, never good, despite the fact that the companies engaging in them do so to make a profit for their owners. Second, no disclosures of *other countries' sanctions* or potential sanctions would be required; the fact that other countries might choose to punish American companies, and thereby also hurt American investors, could just be ignored.

Many groups, as we shall see, have subsequently organized to pressure the SEC into expanding the definition of "material risks" which public companies must disclose to investors, in order to encompass religious, labor, and environmental concerns, and thereby dramatically expand the scope of legal liability which such companies face. The primary targets have been Chinese firms, but Russian firms have also proven popular.

The Deutch Commission went well beyond calling for increased information flows, however. "It is essential," the report states, "that we begin to treat this 'economic warfare' with the same level of sophistication and planning we devote to military options." While noting that the commission "was prohibited in its charter legislation, as amended, from evaluating the adequacy or usefulness of sanctions laws," it nonetheless concluded that "the United States is not making optimal use of its economic leverage" and that "the National Director [for Combating Proliferation] should, in consultation with appropriate agencies and experts from the private sector, assess options for denying proliferators access to U.S. capital markets." This call has since escalated through several congressional bills, which we discuss in this chapter.

The United States–China Security Review Commission

In October 2000, Congress created the twelve-member United States–China Security Review Commission for the purpose of monitoring, investigating, and reporting on the national security implications of the bilateral trade and economic relationship between the United States and China. This commission (which is still in operation) asked the William J. Casey Institute, named for the former CIA director and chaired by one of the panel's members, Roger W. Robinson, Jr., to prepare a report entitled "Capital Markets Transparency and Security: The Nexus Between U.S.–China Security Relations and America's Capital Markets," which we refer to frequently in this chapter. The Casey Institute is operated by the Center for Security Studies, headed by former Assistant Secretary of Defense Frank Gaffney.

The commission's July 2002 report to Congress can only be characterized as relentlessly hostile toward China, chiding its government repeatedly for acting in its own interest rather than America's. The commission even manages to lament the success of China's economic liberalization because of an alleged "adverse impact of recent Chinese economic strength on our Asian allies and friends." The report further reveals that Chinese "[press] coverage of U.S. foreign policy is largely negative and frequently depicts the U.S. as hegemonic and unilateralist" (in contrast to, perhaps, French press coverage?). The report then goes on to lay out a view of U.S. interests that can best be described as hegemonic and recommends a unilateralist agenda for pursuing them.

Part of that agenda is capital markets sanctions. Its primary components are the following.

The commission asked Congress to require the SEC to solicit from foreign issuers information regarding their activities in countries subject to U.S. sanctions and to disclose these to investors. This requirement would hold even where the activities of the issuers were wholly lawful and did not constitute a material risk to investors, according to the SEC staff's judgment. The commission simply stated flatly that such activities were to be branded a material risk, regardless of the SEC's view. Tellingly, no issuers would be required to make comparable disclosures regarding activities in countries subject to sanctions imposed by any *other* countries—no matter which or how many—besides the United States, making transparent the commission's intent to inject politics into the formulation of SEC disclosure standards via a legislated redefinition of materiality.

The commission further wanted the Treasury to assess whether Chinese or other foreign entities "associated with" WMD or missile delivery system proliferation are accessing or seeking to access the U.S. capital markets and to provide this information to the SEC as well as to "investors including state public pension systems and other institutional investors." As the Treasury will not actually be instructed to find evidence of any unlawful activities by foreign companies, this requirement to "inform investors" is clearly intended to dissuade them from buying foreign securities simply through fear of U.S. government retribution.

Finally, the commission asked Congress to bar any Chinese or other foreign entity from issuing securities in the United States if the State Department has imposed sanctions on that entity for engaging in WMD or missile delivery systems proliferation.

The Sudan Peace Act

The 2002 Sudan Peace Act requires the secretary of state to report annually to Congress on the conflict in Sudan. Four specific requirements are laid out. Remarkably, the actual behavior of the Sudanese government, in terms of military action and obstruction of humanitarian relief efforts, comprises only the third and fourth requirements. Numbers one and two relate to the financing of "infrastructure and pipelines for oil exploitation" and "the extent to which that financing was secured in the United States," thus reflecting the passion in the House of Representatives for capital markets sanctions.

The earlier and far more aggressive House version of the act would have barred any company doing business in Sudan from "trading any of its securities" in the United States unless it made specific disclosures, to be dictated to and then formally laid down by the SEC, relating to its activities in Sudan, including "the relationship of the commercial activity to violations of human rights or religious freedom." The House version would further have directed the president to use his authority under the International Emergency Economic Powers Act to bar any company engaged in oil or gas development in Sudan from raising capital or trading its securities in the United States.

The Bush administration opposed these measures in the House bill. In signing the final, Senate- and House-approved version of the act,

President Bush stated that he would interpret its requirements directed at the executive branch only as advisory—this did not sit well in the House. As we shall see in the material that follows, the issue of capital markets sanctions has repeatedly pitted the legislative branch against the executive branch, under both the Clinton and Bush administrations.

Capital Markets Sanctions in Action

In the late 1990s, two cases involving Russian and Chinese oil companies raising capital in the United States brought the issue of capital markets sanctions to the political fore, both in America and abroad. What raised these particular cases to such prominence was the heady mix of large oil firms from countries considered major nemeses by some and partners by others doing business in third countries already subject to highly controversial unilateral U.S. economic sanctions. The cases therefore managed to mobilize politicians, industrial and financial interests, and activists of all stripes in a very public campaign over the merits and feasibility of using the American capital markets as a lever of coercive diplomacy. The campaigns would be celebrated as successes, but the facts bear out a different story.

"Ban the Bond!": The Case of Gazprom

In November 1997, the Russian oil firm Gazprom announced the postponement of a large debt issue in the United States, citing unfavorable market conditions. The decision came two weeks after a stormy Senate Banking Committee hearing at which several members fulminated against the company's investments in Iran and Libya, which had been designated terrorist-sponsoring states by the State Department, as well as its alleged ties with the Russian leadership. Senators Alphonse D'Amato (R-NY), Mitch McConnell (R-KY), Sam Brownback (R-KS), and Lauch Faircloth (R-NC) spoke out strongly in favor of withdrawing long-standing Export-Import Bank guarantees for Gazprom's U.S. suppliers and barring the company from raising private capital in the United States. In the words of Senator Faircloth, "Why should we finance projects for our enemies? I cannot understand anybody with common sense wanting to be part of this deal. I think Wall Street should say 'No' to the deal, and if they do not, then I think we should block it by legislation" (October 3, 1997). The Casey Institute, in its report for the United States—China Security Review Commission, celebrated Gazprom's decision to pull its debt issue as a major victory for the new foreign policy stick they were championing and continue to champion, with passionate supporters in Congress—capital markets sanctions.[9]

But did the threat to deny Gazprom the right to raise capital in the United States actually deny it capital or stop it from doing business in Iran and Libya? Consider first the effect on Gazprom's ability to finance its investments. As the Caseyites tell the tale, Gazprom "withdrew its $3 billion bond offering from the U.S. debt market," the issue having been "derailed" by "debate" over its activities abroad. Although they note that Gazprom raised $3 billion in Europe just a few weeks later, it paid "a higher interest rate" and, "more importantly, a number of Americans likely did not end up underwriting a company partnering with a terrorist-sponsoring state in violation of U.S. law." Unfortunately, this is a tall tale. Here is what actually happened.

Gazprom's U.S. convertible bond issue was only $1 billion, a third the size claimed by the Caseyites. An additional $2 billion in *Eurobond* issues had been planned for 1998. (To put these figures in context, Gazprom's market capitalization was near $70 billion at the time.) As for the notion that Gazprom halted the U.S. issue in response to noises from Congress, the facts lend no support. Even D'Amato's own staff made no such claim.[10]

Gazprom's chairman, Rem Vyakhirev, was robust in responding to threats of U.S. capital markets sanctions: "We do not take part in political games and are only pursuing commercial goals. The development of the gas resources on the Gulf shelf has nothing to do with supporting international terrorism. It is impermissible to threaten Gazprom with sanctions."[11] Gazprom halted its bond offering because market demand for Russian securities had turned sharply negative in the wake of global market sell-offs in the few weeks prior, in particular a 30 percent fall in the Russian stock market (which hit Gazprom's London-traded shares). Along with Gazprom, Russia's Taftnet also announced that it was delaying a U.S. securities issue (an American Depositary Receipt, or ADR) owing to market conditions. Furthermore, Gazprom had simultaneously announced postponement of *both* the U.S. *and* Eurobond issues as well as an intention to proceed with them if and when market conditions improved in 1998. As the *Financial Times* explained it, "Emerging market countries are switching to the syndicated loan markets to compensate for the dramatic cost of issuing bonds since turmoil hit the global markets in late October."[12] More than 40 emerging market borrowers had postponed or cancelled planned international bond issues in the two weeks prior to Gazprom's decision.

As for the Export-Import Bank loan guarantees, Gazprom unilaterally canceled its arrangement with the agency, its spokesman saying that "this step was taken in order to prevent the use of the American bank's guarantees on supplies of oil and gas equipment as a way of putting pressure on Russian companies implementing projects abroad."[13] A Voice of Russia radio commentary put it more bluntly: "Gazprom decided to annul the agreement with the Export-Import Bank of the USA to pre-empt any discriminatory measures by the bank. So who is the loser? The equipment which Gazprom intended to buy in the United States is not special. It can be found in other countries as well. And now that the agreement has been annulled, the American companies which planned to sign big contracts with Gazprom have lost a good customer. The reputation of the U.S. government's bank has suffered. Washington's attempts to impose its rules of conduct on the world trade market have failed."[14]

But what about Gazprom having to raise the $3 billion "at a higher interest rate" just a few weeks later in Europe? Was this not at least a partial success for U.S. capital markets sanctions?

Not at all. First, the debt raised in Europe was not a replacement for the U.S. convertible bond issue, as the Caseyites claimed. A $3 billion European syndicated loan had been announced in August 1997, as a complement to the U.S. convertible bond and Eurobond issues, four months before the bond issues were shelved.[15] Thus the story painting the European loan as a high-priced substitute for the U.S. bond issue is pure fiction. Second, the "higher interest rate" claim is as meaningless as it is undocumented.[16] A straight loan naturally carries a higher interest rate than a bond convertible into stock. Furthermore, by any standard Gazprom's European loan was a major success. With an eight-year maturity, it was priced at a mere 1.75 percent over the benchmark "Libor" interest rate—or 0.25 percent *less* than Gazprom had paid in April, when *Euromoney* raved about "Gazprom's stunning loan debut."[17] By way of comparison, it would have cost Gazprom more than 4 percent over Libor to borrow in Russia.[18]

So blackballing Gazprom from the U.S. bond market did precisely nothing to affect the company's financing strategy or its cost. But did it not at least keep Americans from "underwriting a company partnering with a terrorist-sponsoring state"?

Once again, no. The fact that the loan was organized "in Europe" says nothing about the nationality of the capital. And neither do the Caseyites, who are either unaware of or simply choose to ignore the participation of major American banks in the loan. Citibank and Bankers Trust were underwriters, suggesting, according to the *Financial Times,* that "US banks have not been deterred from doing business with Gazprom in spite of threats of US government retaliation against the company because of its plans to invest in Iran."[19]

Finally, then, consider the effect on Gazprom's operations in Iran, the actual target of the sanctions threats. In a letter to Vice President Al Gore dated October 8, 1997, Senator D'Amato and Representative Benjamin Gilman (R-NY), defending the efficacy of sanctions, asked rhetorically, "In view of Gazprom's recent very large tax payments to the government and its extensive need for capital to modernize its domestic and Euro gas networks, where would it find the resources to fund this natural gas contract?"

It found the resources. Six weeks after the letter was sent, Gazprom announced it would invest $600 million in the development of Iran's South Pars gas field, its deputy chairman stating that the company was "absolutely indifferent" to objections raised in the United States.[20] In May 1998, the Clinton administration waived sanctions under the Iran–Libya Sanctions Act against Gazprom and its Iran project partners, Total of France and Petronas of Malaysia, after concluding that they would have no effect on investment, while making it more difficult to gain Russian and European cooperation on other foreign policy matters.[21] Secretary of State Madeleine Albright indicated that the "waivers will prevent retaliation against U.S. firms, which the imposition of sanctions would probably engender, and avoid possible challenges based on claims related to treaties and other international obligations."[22] By July 2004, Gazprom and its partners had completed development of the $2 billion complex in South Pars, which would net Gazprom 41.15 billion cubic meters of gas and a guaranteed 16.8 percent return on investment over seven years after the start of production.[23]

The Casey Institute considers this to be a case study in successful sanctions. We leave the reader to ponder what failure might have looked like.

"Not on My Market!": The Case of PetroChina

In September 1999, the first reports emerged that the China National Petroleum Company (CNPC) planned to list on the New York Stock Exchange (NYSE), raising between $5 billion and $10 billion in equity capital. The proposed offering provoked strong objections from members of Congress, notably Representative Frank Wolf (R-VA), based largely on CNPC's business in Sudan. CNPC had invested about $1.5 billion in the Sudanese energy sector and had reportedly committed multiples of that to future exploration and development in the country. Opponents of CNPC's New York listing claimed it would assist the government in Khartoum in prolonging an 18-year-old civil war which they alleged had caused two million deaths and displaced twice as many.

CNPC, apparently reacting to the political tempest in the United States, restructured itself such that only a subsidiary entity—PetroChina, from which Sudanese and other non-Chinese assets were excluded— would list on the NYSE. The move—referred to on Wall Street as a Chinese Wall—infuriated CNPC's American detractors, who saw it as a meaningless bit of legal maneuvering to safeguard the U.S. listing while allowing the Sudanese operations to develop unhindered.

The American public campaign against PetroChina's U.S. initial public offering (IPO) was waged primarily by congressmen at the conservative and liberal ends of the spectrum, former Republican government officials, organizations associated with the Christian Right, the AFL-CIO, a protectionist small-business lobby group called the U.S. Business and Industrial Council, and the Casey Institute. Whereas most of PetroChina's detractors expressed concern for human and religious rights in Sudan, they were united only in their loathing of China. Even here, however, there was no agreement among them. The AFL-CIO report, for example, "pointedly . . . ignored the national security concerns raised by the conservative elements of the informal coalition,"[24] in the words of one of the report's authors, choosing to focus instead on Chinese labor market conditions. Others, such as Congressmen Dennis Kucinich (D-OH) and Bernard Sanders (Socialist-VT) were exercised over potential environmental damage in Tibet.

The labor group turned out to be PetroChina's only potent enemy in the United States. Although President Clinton and SEC Chairman Arthur Levitt refused political or regulatory intervention, the AFL-CIO was able to bring its influence to bear directly on the investment policies of certain fund management firms. With tens of billions of dollars of their members' pension fund assets under union control, the AFL-CIO was able to back its position with big bucks and board seats. A coalition of labor trustees and friendly Democratic political appointments (such as San Francisco Mayor Willie Brown) on the board of the California Public Employees' Retirement System (CalPERS) succeeded not only in blocking the giant pension fund from investing in the PetroChina IPO, but in rewriting CalPERS's investment policies so as to impose emerging market "investibility screens" based on factors such as labor practices. The national teachers' and professors' pension fund TIAA-CREF also announced that it would not take a stake in the company.

The PetroChina IPO was ultimately scaled down to $2.89 billion, which the Casey Institute attributed wholly to the efforts of the U.S. anti-PetroChina campaign. Many contemporaneous news reports, however, do not even mention the campaign in explaining the scale-back, focusing instead, as in the *Financial Times,* on U.S. institutional investor concern over "problems associated with Chinese state companies: huge workforces, inefficiency, poor management control, and debt."[25] The company's preliminary listing prospectus could not have excited investors by declaring that the bulk of the IPO proceeds were earmarked for "debt repayment and severance compensation."[26] Other reports mentioned the market's fascination with technology offerings at the time, which led Beijing to put greater priority on Internet and telecoms issues thereafter.[27]

The Caseyites end their tale of the great victory achieved by "the tireless efforts of those in the 'PetroChina Coalition' and concerned

Members of Congress"[28] by crediting them with an 8 percent fall in PetroChina's share price between the company's IPO on March 31, 2000, and its first-day NYSE close on April 6. They do not mention that the stock was the second most actively traded on the Big Board in its debut, the price ending the day virtually unchanged.

The epilogue, however, turns out to be far more telling than the tale.

Over the past four years CNPC has become the major force in the Sudanese oil industry, having been wholly undeterred by the efforts to bar it from the U.S. capital markets. By 2002, China was Sudan's most important customer. About 75 percent of Sudan's exports is petroleum products, and 85 percent of such products go to China via CNPC. By 2003, CNPC's production base in Sudan accounted for nearly half the company's overseas oil production, making Sudan China's fourth largest oil supplier. At an average price per barrel of $26.70 for Sudanese oil in 2003, we calculate that CNPC's 2003 equity oil production of 5.67 million tons was worth $1.11 billion. A proprietary estimate we have seen puts CNPC's remaining Sudan project value at $2.126 billion as of the beginning of 2004, giving the company a post-tax rate of return of 39.7 percent. CNPC's 90 percent stake in PetroChina translated into a $4 billion dividend for the parent in 2004, helping to fuel its international expansion.[29]

By January 2004, PetroChina's share price had quadrupled—powerful testimony to the utter irrelevance of the capital markets sanctions campaign either to the company's business strategy or its performance. In the end, the coalition's "tireless efforts" changed nothing in China and nothing in Sudan. But the good news is that PetroChina's American investors never actually suffered from the "political risk" the Caseyites claimed to be so eager to protect them from—although millions of teachers, professors, and California public sector workers never shared in the windfall, their pension funds having declined to buy the stock.

The notion that CNPC would have sacrificed its huge Sudan business for an NYSE listing is ludicrous. Using data from JPMorgan's ADR.com, we calculated that as of August 2003 the value of U.S. institutional holdings in PetroChina stock was *twice as large in Hong Kong as it was in New York*. In other words, not only was PetroChina *capable* of attracting U.S. capital through the Hong Kong Stock Exchange, but it actually proved *more successful* in attracting it through Hong Kong than New York. Warren Buffett, not normally considered to be a naive investor, controls nearly 14 percent of publicly traded PetroChina shares, and 95 percent of his stake is held through purchases on the Hong Kong Stock Exchange.[30] The Casey Institute finds it "difficult to imagine U.S. investors flocking to the stock of a targeted firm in the event that company lists overseas."[31] Yet this is precisely what happened.

With the exception of union and politically controlled funds, fund managers, who are hired and fired based on financial performance, seek stocks with the highest expected returns and seek to buy them where they are cheapest. In the case of Hong Kong–listed stocks, fund managers told us that it was almost invariably cheapest to buy there because of the critical liquidity from the Asian investor base.

The best way to understand the significance of this finding is to consider that the savings to CNPC's cost of capital owing to its NYSE listing amounts to mere pocket change, particularly when viewed side by side with the cash flow deriving from its Sudan business. Now, actually to imagine that the United States could persuade the regime in Khartoum to cease actions it considers vital to holding power by barring a Chinese oil firm from listing on the NYSE is to elevate imagination well beyond any legitimate role it should play in foreign policy formulation.

The image of religious freedom watchdogs, China hawks, Tibetan independence advocates, unionists, and environmentalists all joining hands—"the Sudan Community," as the Caseyites call this eclectic kumbaya collection—to oppose foreign investment in Sudan is both misleading and disingenuous. Prominent human rights advocates *actually living in Sudan* had been extremely critical of a June 2001 House bill (an embryonic version of the 2002 Sudan Peace Act) aimed at punishing foreign oil companies doing business in the country. "This isolation by the international community for nine years did not work," according to Rifaat Makkawi, a Khartoum-based human rights lawyer. The bill, had it passed the Senate, would have forced the Canadian oil firm Talisman Energy to sell its stake in a Sudanese joint venture or delist from the New York Stock Exchange. "If Talisman were to pull out of Sudan, this doesn't mean the oil business will come to an end," said the jailed Sudanese human rights lawyer Ghazi Suleiman. Talisman, which had quietly pressed human rights concerns on a Sudanese government over which the West had little other leverage, according to Sudanese opposition figures, would merely be replaced by other companies, wholly outside U.S. jurisdiction and much less susceptible to Western public pressure to consider the impact of their actions on the Sudanese people.[32] "The way forward is not to take away companies . . . that have been working to end some of the abuse," said Alfred Taban, publisher of Khartoum's only independent newspaper. In fact, the leading candidates to buy out the Talisman stake were Chinese, Sudanese, and Malaysian state oil companies. With these ready suitors in mind, Sudan's finance minister reacted to passage of the House bill by stating that Talisman's departure would make no difference to the government.[33]

A few material financial facts on Talisman. At the time of writing in August 2004, 77 percent of the year's trading volume in Talisman stock occurred on the Toronto Stock Exchange, and only 20 percent on the NYSE, despite the fact that nearly half of the company's shareholder base is American. In April 2002, Talisman raised $569 million in 15-year notes through the London-based European debt markets. The issue was two-thirds larger than originally anticipated, owing to higher than expected demand. "This is the largest debt issue ever completed by Talisman and serves to broaden our fixed income investor base beyond North America," said Talisman's CEO, Jim Buckee. The move to London was clearly intended to sidestep any further financial threats against the company in the United States and vindicated Alan Greenspan's July 2000 congressional testimony in which he argued that U.S. capital markets sanctions would merely push capital raising to London.[34] These facts should illustrate that, even for a firm with a heavy U.S. ownership base, driving more trading abroad will not aid U.S. foreign policy aims one iota.

Has the government in Khartoum repented for the sins which led to passage of the 2001 House bill? Hardly. In 2004 the regime was the target of widespread charges of complicity in ethnic cleansing and genocide in the western region of Darfur, where an estimated 50,000 people died and 1.2 million fled their homes. Preventing such a humanitarian disaster would have required dedicated and muscular diplomacy. America chose instead to bludgeon foreign companies with threats of sanctions—for-

eign companies being a soft political target, with no domestic con-
stituency—and failed in so doing to achieve any political aims within
Sudan.

If impotence were the only indictment that could be leveled against
capital markets sanctions, they might be overlooked as a relatively harmless political pressure valve, occupying politicians so that they don't do
something considerably more rash or counterproductive. As we discuss
below, however, such sanctions campaigns have the potential to cause
considerable collateral damage to America's regulatory and capital-
raising infrastructure.

Hijacking the SEC

[The U.S. Markets Security Act] calls for a national security office within
the SEC. . . . Now why is this necessary? It is responsive both to current
trends and forward looking to the age when economic warfare may
supersede more traditional forms of warfare.
                       —Representative Gerald Solomon (R-NY)[35]

On April 2, 2001, Congressman Frank Wolf wrote a letter to SEC
Acting Chairman Laura Unger excoriating PetroChina and Talisman for
"offenses" in relation to their activities in Sudan. "While other governmental agencies have jurisdiction over human rights, national security
and other related abuses in Sudan," he said, "in this case *it is corporations
with securities that have been offered to U.S. investors,* not governments,
that have committed offenses." "For that reason," he continued, "the
SEC, with its authority and mandate to oversee disclosure to inform and
protect investors, should recognize material omissions by the companies
as a violation of their disclosure requirements and take appropriate
action." He then laid out a laundry list of investment "risks" which
PetroChina failed to reveal in its filings. Among these omissions, "The
prospectus contained no accounting of the massive public opposition
campaign levied against PetroChina," of which Wolf was a part, "and the
potential risk to investors of this ongoing activism on share value"—a risk
not immediately apparent in the stock's 17 percent rise over the year
between its NYSE launch and the date of Congressman Wolf's letter, or
the 300 percent rise by the beginning of 2004.

Congressman Wolf's main aim in writing this letter, as well as one the previous month urging Unger to take action to delist PetroChina from the NYSE,[36] was clear: to bring American political influence to bear to stop foreign companies from doing business in Sudan. While controversial on several levels, this is certainly a legitimate *object* of American foreign policy. The SEC, however, is not a legitimate *instrument* of American foreign policy.

The SEC plays a vital role in the American capital markets as a neutral arbiter of competition rules and protector of investor financial interests. This role is exemplified in a senior staff memo prepared for Unger, in response to the Wolf letter, in the section dealing with "materiality" in disclosure rules:

> The question of whether disclosure is required will depend on the materiality of the financial impact of those operations and business relationships on the company's conduct of its business. SEC disclosure rules and policies turn on the concept of materiality. The Supreme Court has held that information is material "if there is a substantial likelihood that a reasonable shareholder would consider it important in making an investment decision." *TSC Industries v. Northway Inc.*, 426 U.S. 438, 449 (1976).
>
> *In assessing materiality, the SEC staff takes the view that the reasonable investor generally focuses on matters that have affected, or will affect, a company's profitability and financial outlook.*[37] (emphasis added)

That is, the SEC assesses materiality on the basis of its relevance to investor financial interests. The SEC's role is not to advise investors about what is good for them—let alone what might be good for the United States—or even to educate investors regarding ethical, religious, or foreign policy matters which may attach to doing business overseas. These matters may well be assigned, through appropriate legislation, to other arms of government but ill-suit an agency whose reputation for integrity across the globe is intimately bound up with its ability to remain scrupulously neutral in questions as to which businesses do and do not "deserve" private capital. This reputation is critical to America's ability to attract capital markets activity within its legal jurisdiction.

Unfortunately, Unger reacted to Wolf's letter by dropping what the *Financial Times* termed a "bombshell."[38] Despite making clear to the congressman that foreign companies doing business in countries subject to U.S. sanctions,[39] such as Sudan, were neither subject to those sanctions nor in any way barred from offering their stock in the United States, she concluded that "the SEC does, however, have statutory authority to require that U.S. investors receive adequate disclosure about where the proceeds of their securities investments are going and how they are being used," regardless of whether such disclosure were merited by her own staff's assessment of materiality. She further revealed that she and members of her staff had met with the director and staff of the State Department's Office of International Religious Freedom, with which she had personally raised "the possibility of interagency cooperation on Sudan."[40] (Perhaps they also discussed the plight of Scientologists in Germany, and how the SEC might alleviate it by badgering German companies listed in New York?) Unger's behavior marked a sharp departure from that of her predecessor, Arthur Levitt, who, like President Clinton, declined entreaties from congressmen to block or delay the PetroChina IPO.

Of the now-famous Unger letter, Casey Institute Chairman Roger Robinson said it "could represent a sea change in the way in which foreign registrants access the US capital markets. . . . National security, human rights and religious freedom concerns are now regarded as material risk to investors."[41] Indeed, in rendering a "material risk" any activity of a foreign company that the SEC could be successfully pressured to so label, there was literally no limit to the scope of foreign policy opinions (and opinions they are, as no legislation or executive order is necessary) which pressure groups could champion through the SEC's disclosure, investigation, enforcement—and, now, "interagency cooperation"—regimes.

How would groups successfully exert pressure on the SEC to bring politics to bear in its operations? Through the appropriations process. In 1999, Representatives Spencer Bachus (R-AL) and Dennis Kucinich failed in their attempt to revive a 1997 effort to pass a U.S. Markets Security Act, which would have created an Office of National Security within the SEC. However, in March 2004, speaking before the House committee responsible for the SEC's funding, SEC Chairman William Donaldson revealed that a new Office of Global Security Risk (OGSR) had been created within the commission to "identify companies whose activities raise concern about global security risks that are material to investors" and to investigate them and share relevant information with other government agencies.[42] That committee was chaired by none other than Congressman Wolf, who spearheaded the office's creation and inserted its mandate into the committee's July 2003 SEC appropriations recommendation.

The mandate, which requires companies listed on U.S. exchanges to disclose whether they are doing business in states designated by the State Department as sponsoring terrorism, links the State Department list to SEC oversight by stating that the requirements are based on "the risk to corporate share value and reputation stemming from business interests in these higher risk countries" and thereby override SEC materiality judgments. President Bush in signing the appropriations bill pointed out that accompanying reports "do not have the force of law" and "are not legally binding," but Wolf's spokesman made clear that "it's now the law and he expects [the SEC] to abide by it."[43]

It is important to recognize that if Congress wishes to bar Americans from making certain investments it has it within its power to do so directly—by passing legislation. Congress could also try to persuade the White House to issue executive orders. The fact that Congressman Wolf and others choose instead to pursue their agenda through the SEC represents a dangerous misuse of that agency in the service of an agenda they could not persuade their fellow elected officials to enact.

What's Risk to the Goose Is Risk to the Gander

Reporting on the creation of the OGSR, the *International Enforcement Law Reporter* concluded that "the program's effectiveness and the potential for diversion of investment outside the U.S. will depend in large degree on whether other governments develop and implement in a similar fashion and with similar resources such a program. Unilateral measures will lead to foreign companies diverting their investment away from the U.S. or reorganizing commercial structures to accommodate the new office."[44] Is there any evidence supporting this conclusion?

In July 2001, the large Russian oil company Lukoil reacted to the Unger letter by withdrawing its planned share listing on the NYSE, choosing to move it instead to the London Stock Exchange, citing the "political risk" now associated with an American listing. The relentless badgering of the SEC to politicize its disclosure requirements, under the guise of informing investors of "political risk" in foreign investments, had succeeded in *creating* political risk in American listings, driving capital-seeking companies outside the SEC's jurisdiction entirely, where they continue to access U.S. as well as foreign capital. Indeed, every major U.S. investment bank is a member of the London Stock Exchange, which operates electronically and can receive and execute trading orders from around the world almost as fast as a trader can blink.

Lukoil's decision was nonetheless celebrated by Frank Gaffney in a *Washington Times* op ed as a "development of momentous significance."[45] Of far greater significance is the dangerous level of ignorance within parts of the U.S. defense and intelligence establishment as to the workings of the capital markets, given that some of their notables have been turning to the most foolish possible forms of market regulation as a substitute for real foreign policy.

Activists of All Stripes Climb on the Bandwagon

We are very concerned that the creation of this Office [of Global Security Risk] could be a first step towards politicizing the U.S. capital markets and would set a bad policy precedent. The establishment of such an office could also create troubling issues relating to the SEC's traditional and time-honored standards of disclosure and "materiality." We fear that if an office dealing specifically sanctions issues were created within the SEC, then it may not be long before other political or social issues are judged sufficiently important to justify the creation of separate offices within the Commission dedicated to their protection.
—Letter to SEC Chairman William Donaldson from Securities Industry Association President Mark Lackritz (January 20, 2004)

Was Lackritz fear-mongering?

It appears not. Environmentalists have now jumped on the capital markets bandwagon, seeing securities regulation as a useful tool for expanding environmental regulation both within and across borders. A recent report of an intergovernmental commission, for example, proposed obliging all public companies to take on new "disclosure requirements related to environmental protection,"[46] whether or not such disclosures had any relevance to investment risks.

The Commission for Environmental Cooperation was established as a complement to the North American Free Trade Agreement (NAFTA) to address environmental issues "arising in the context of liberalized trade." The commission contracted three environmentalists—one each from the United States, Canada, and Mexico—to prepare a report on environmental disclosure requirements in the securities regulations and financial accounting standards of the three countries. Their 2002 report breaks new legal ground in attempting to redefine the legal understanding of materiality in financial disclosure requirements such that items that are financially immaterial become material solely by virtue of their being related to the environment.

The SEC Staff Accounting Bulletin on Materiality (1999), cited extensively in the report, states that "materiality concerns the significance of an item to users of a registrant's financial statement." Yet the NAFTA commission's report boldly declares "that it is explicit that information bearing on the competence or integrity of management, including noncompliance with extant laws and regulations, can be material *even if financially insignificant*" (emphasis added).[47] How did it reach such a startling judgment?

The report starts by appealing to the 1969 U.S. National Environmental Protection Act (NEPA), which, in section 102(1), states that NEPA "directs that, to the fullest extent possible, the policies, regulations, and public laws of the United States shall be interpreted and administered in accordance with the policies set forth in this act." On the basis of this single sentence, the report concludes that "Congress thereby authorized and directed the Securities and Exchange Commission, as a federal agency, to include environmental protection in its mandate to issue regulations in the public interest."

So the report has now added environmental protection to the SEC's bailiwick. This the NAFTA commission then relates to corporate financial statements by claiming that the SEC staff say that "misstatements or omissions . . . might be material although quantitatively small in financial terms. Among these are misstatements bearing on the integrity or competence of management, *such as a company's compliance with environmental regulatory requirements*" (emphasis added).[48]

Is this correct? Does the SEC really take the view that a company's compliance with all environmental regulations is material to investors and therefore must be fully disclosed in financial statements, even if there is no alleged wrongdoing and no financial significance to such disclosures?

Not at all. The bulletin states that "as a result of the interaction of quantitative and qualitative considerations in materiality judgments, misstatements of relatively small amounts . . . could have a material effect on the financial statements." It then goes on to give examples of quantitatively small misstatements of fact—such as a misstatement that "masks a change in earnings or other trends"—that could have a quantitatively large effect on financial statements. In other words, the report's claim that the SEC considers environmental disclosures to be material even if financially insignificant is pure nonsense. In fact, the bulletin says absolutely nothing whatsoever about "a company's compliance with environmental regulatory requirements." Despite a farrago of misstatements about U.S. capital market regulation, the report manages to conclude that across the three countries "upward harmonization of enforcement activities [related to 'environmental disclosure'] would be consistent with NAFTA's investment and sustainable development objectives."

But could reports like this really foreshadow new lawsuits and legal liability for companies listing in the United States? In March 2004, following creation of the OGSR, 13 state and municipal treasurers and labor pension funds wrote to Chairman Donaldson asking the commission to require companies to make more detailed environmental risk disclosures, focusing in particular on climate risk. Crain's *Investment News* pointed to the letter and to the legislation requiring establishment of the OGSR as examples of the SEC coming "under increasing pressure to demand more detailed analysis of environmental, social and other risks by public companies." Financial advisers expected more lawsuits and liability in consequence: and as one commented, "How do you prove that you're not harming the environment?"[49]

Environmental activists act properly when they press for legal restrictions on environmentally damaging activities. Seeking to control the SEC's materiality standard, however, is wholly inappropriate, as such behavior is intended to impose new corporate legal liabilities through the back door rather than simply to ensure that existing material liabilities are revealed—something which the SEC already requires.

The AFL-CIO has used shareholder activism as leverage to support labor causes far and wide; for example, to back German unions in opposition to Vodafone's takeover of Mannesman and to protest Burmese labor practices by leading divestiture campaigns.[50] The track record of these capital markets campaigns is poor, but they are nonetheless wholly legitimate means of expressing the organization's views on how and where money should and should not be invested (assuming, of course, that their members support having their pension fund assets used as "social investment" vehicles). How union members choose lawfully to invest, or not to invest, their pension money is clearly their business. Ditto for their right to try to persuade others to invest, or not to invest, as they do.

Such campaigns stand in stark contrast, however, to efforts to use the SEC and public company disclosure regulations to force non-U.S. companies to declare publicly that one or another group's foreign or social policy concerns represent "risks" to investing in those companies' securities, for which those companies should henceforth be held legally liable. The only reason supporters of capital markets sanctions demand such forced disclosures is that their concerns do not meet the materiality standard for determining *all* risks that must be disclosed to investors; this standard being one of the cornerstones of the American investor protection regime. If their concerns did meet this standard, then specific new disclosure requirements would obviously be redundant.

Of Sanctions and Sausage

> Anyone who likes sanctions or sausage should watch neither one being made.

Otto von Bismarck's famous analogy actually referred to legislation rather than sanctions. Yet the two typically bear great similarity in terms of the way in which they are crafted and sold. In this final section, we take an unexpurgated look at the blood, fat, and gristle of capital markets sanctions.

Is This Really About Risks to Investors?

As we have already explained, the SEC is chartered to protect American investor interests. It is not chartered to protect, let alone advance, American foreign policy interests. Recognizing these limitations, some proponents of capital markets sanctions have adopted a different line of reasoning: these sanctions actually protect investors from the "material risk factors in the markets that can depress the value of certain foreign securities." Conveniently, these "higher risks" are specifically associated with investing in entities they designate as "global bad actors."[51] No one has been a more vocal promoter of this argument than the Casey Institute.

William J. Casey, having been both director of the CIA and chairman of the SEC, has proven posthumously to be a highly effective celebrity in rallying acolytes for a particularly aggressive form of financial statecraft. And the institute that bears his name has consistently sought to fuse finance and foreign policy to the point where the former becomes little more than a servant of a peculiarly hawkish version of the latter. In so doing, they have co-opted the language of financial regulation in such a manner that any foreign business of which they disapprove can and should automatically be branded by the U.S. government as a "bad investment."

When considering the institute's argument, it is critical to recognize that the SEC already requires that company prospectuses and annual reports "describe *any risk attendant to the foreign operations* and any dependence on one or more of the registrant's segments upon such foreign operations"[52] (emphasis added), meaning that new regulations targeted at non-U.S. firms engaged in lawful activities in a foreign country can only be intended to harm the ability of those firms to market securities in the United States, and not to protect American investors.

At least as relevant, "bad" activities do not equate with higher risk any more than "good" activities equate with lower risk. Securities of companies doing business in a country subject to U.S. sanctions may be spectacularly good investment opportunities, particularly as such companies face no competition from U.S. firms. (And if it is a material risk for investors, SEC regulations already require that the companies reveal it.)

The argument that bad actors might still be good investments is so obvious that even the Casey Institute cannot avoid making it occasionally. Consider what Chairman Robinson says about traditional economic sanctions: "The use of economic sanctions as a policy tool is under unprecedented attack on Capitol Hill and elsewhere. This is primarily because our allies have little or no interest in joining us in the multilateral application of such sanctions and the global business community is strenuously opposed to the *loss of exports, profits and jobs which generally accompany security-minded sanctions*" (emphasis added).[53] If "security-minded sanctions" generally lead to profit losses, then the activities being targeted by sanctions must obviously be profitable for shareholders. Logically, one cannot have it both ways.

Through his company, Conflict Securities, however, Robinson appears to be trying to. It markets a "Global Security Risk Monitor" to institutional investors, which supposedly helps them to "assess the portfolio risks associated with corporate ties to terrorist-sponsoring nations and the proliferation of weapons of mass destruction and ballistic missile delivery systems." CalPERS dropped the product at the end of 2002 after a staff memo to its investment committee indicated that its contents "bear no real insights into risk related to terrorism or national security."[54] This is not surprising, as Robinson is not actually concerned with investment risk, even if he is not averse to earning a living from slapping the label on companies whose activities he disapproves of.

And what about the securities of companies doing business in a country subject to, or potentially subject to, other countries' sanctions? Could these not be bad investments for Americans?

Imagine the SEC mandating the following disclosure in Halliburton's financial statements: "Halliburton currently has major contractual commitments with the U.S. military in Iraq. Many countries around the world deem Iraq to be occupied by the U.S. military, an institution that has been involved in documented human rights abuses in the country's Abu Ghraib prison. This may have serious negative consequences for the company's ability to conduct business in many parts of the world." Needless to say, Robinson has never called for the SEC to impose such disclosure obligations on American companies. We suspect he would be appalled if they did.

Supporters of capital markets sanctions deliberately conflate investment risk with "risks" related to such matters as weapons proliferation, religious persecution, labor exploitation, and environmental degradation in order to co-opt securities law and regulation in the service of narrow foreign policy agendas for which they cannot muster legislative or executive branch support. The danger is that they will succeed—not in achieving their foreign policy aims, but in politicizing American capital market regulation to the point where it is irrelevant to foreign firms, as the activity will have migrated to London and other nonpoliticized jurisdictions.

Is This Really About Defending the National Interest?

The United States' bilateral strategic relationship with China is arguably the most important in the post–Cold War world, and should not be disrupted by what are ultimately second-order issues that can be addressed in other ways.

—RAND analyst James Mulvenon[55]

As Roger Robinson would have it, unilateral American capital markets sanctions against Chinese, Russian, and other foreign companies are needed because traditional economic sanctions don't work when applied unilaterally, and our allies won't back us multilaterally. As we have already seen, however, unilateral capital markets sanctions don't work any better than unilateral economic sanctions. In fact, they are even less effective because of the fungibility of money. (The inability to buy a fighter plane from Texas may mean having to buy an inferior one from Argenteuil, but dollars can be borrowed on almost identical terms in New York and London.) As for the failings of America's allies, this plays nicely with the domestic political segment which enjoys painting America as uniquely principled and unswerving when confronted by other sovereign wills, and her allies as consistently weak, accommodating, and venal.

In reality, however, the much deeper drama is being played out entirely at home. Six successive U.S. administrations, from Nixon through Bush II, have sought to engage China constructively and have resisted, often at significant political cost, attempts in Congress to impose a hard line on trade and security matters. We believe this approach has been heartily vindicated by the emergence of an enormous Chinese middle class—the economic backbone of the world's second-largest importing nation—with a powerful interest in deepening commercial relations and mitigating political conflict with America and her Asian allies, particularly Japan and South Korea. We also see the passion with which the capital markets sanctions movement has been engaged in the United States as a reflection of the consistent failure of its supporters to win the political argument at home.

Where Is "American Capital"?

The principal advantage of turning increasingly to financial sanctions—as opposed to trade sanctions—is that access to the U.S. capital markets will likely prove essential for large-scale foreign entities like those of China and generally does not involve any underlying exports or jobs. . . . With the largest share of the world's available development capital domiciled in New York City, we have in our possession the kind of leverage that, if used prudently and constructively, can make the United States and our allies more secure in the 21st century, even if employed unilaterally.

Casey Institute Chairman Roger W. Robinson, Jr.[56]

The notion that American capital is "domiciled in New York City" is dangerously naïve. American capital may be owned by Americans, but it is effectively undomiciled.

Studying JP Morgan ADR.com data for 2003, we found that for 122 EU-based firms listing ADRs on the NYSE, U.S. institutional investors held, on average for each company, 7.7 times as much of the underlying stock listed in Europe as they did of the ADRs. For mainland Chinese firms, the ratio of U.S. institutional holdings in Hong Kong to holdings on the NYSE is 5.8.[57]

The clear message from these data is that *U.S. investors go abroad to invest.* They do not sit in New York City waiting for the world to come to them (at Robinson's pleasure). Critically, American capital markets sanctions can only accelerate this trend. If foreign firms are barred or discouraged from raising American capital within America's legal jurisdiction, they will simply raise it outside—as Lukoil and Gazprom did. The only effective way to bar foreign companies from accessing American capital is to bar American investors from providing it.

But Could Capital Markets Sanctions Be Made to Work?

The forces of arbitrage across investments and across borders make it nearly impossible for any government to raise the cost of capital to a given foreign firm such that that firm would, on that basis, abandon what it considered to be a major strategic business activity. The cost of capital for investments of comparable riskiness tends strongly to equalize across financial centers. It is therefore inconceivable that all capable firms could be so starved of capital that they would forswear the targeted activity and thereby allow foreign policy aims to be achieved through capital markets sanctions.

Take an example. The stillborn U.S. "China Non-Proliferation Act" of 2000 contained provisions that would have allowed the president to bar Chinese companies from raising debt or equity capital in the United States. "This is leverage," said one of its sponsors, Senator Fred Thompson (R-TN), "perhaps enough to cause China to reconsider some of those missile sales" to countries such as Iran, North Korea, and Pakistan. Could this be true?

According to the Casey Institute, which strongly supported this legislation, twenty-five basis points (0.25%) would be a significant premium to bear for borrowing one way rather than another "when borrowing multibillion-dollar sums."[58] Let us therefore say that a Chinese state-controlled company engaged in missile proliferation were, on the basis of this legislation, to be obliged to move a huge $2 billion bond deal from New York to London, suffering a twenty-five basis point penalty in the process. What would this cost the company?

The answer is a mere $5 million. Would such a company, with the potential to earn hundreds of millions of dollars annually from cross-border missile sales, and in pursuit of Chinese government policy, cease such sales in order to save twenty-five basis points on a bond issue? If that seems unlikely, now imagine how unlikely it would be for all of that firm's competitors, on the basis of that firm being prohibited from selling bonds in New York, to be deterred from selling missiles abroad. And only if all of them could be so deterred could capital markets sanctions achieve their foreign policy aim: to stop missile proliferation.

If American investments in certain enterprises do truly represent a material security risk to Americans, then Congress and the president should apply their ample powers to ban them altogether. Their efforts should be targeted at obliging Americans to divest from, and not invest in, companies that meet such a security-risk standard, rather than at encouraging such companies merely to access American capital in foreign jurisdictions. The reason they have not done so in the cases of Chinese, Russian, and other companies discussed in this chapter is that supporters of such bans have simply failed to muster sufficient support for legislation or executive orders. And they have failed because enough of their colleagues have recognized the negligible benefits and enormous countervailing risks that would be posed to the American capital markets; to the preservation of a rules-based system of international commerce and capital flows, upon which American prosperity and security depend; and to American diplomatic influence in the world from blanket investment bans and forced divestitures, particularly if these appear to foreign firms and governments, as well as to American investors, to be applied unreasonably or indiscriminately.

But What's Wrong With Transparency?

We now have a new proposal . . . called the China Nonproliferation Act, that was introduced by Senator Thompson, that seeks for the first time to use access to our capital market and banking system as an instrument of American foreign policy. The objectives of the bill are objectives that no one can disagree with, and that is, we would like nations not to proliferate in terms of weapon sales. But the tools that are being used represent, in my opinion, a very real threat to our prosperity.

Senator Phil Gramm[59]

Some have even raised the argument that the transparency provision in our bill is bad and will do great harm to our capital markets. . . . Is it so bad to let American investors know that their hard-earned dollars might be providing capital to support a weapons proliferation program for North Korea or Libya that might one day threaten their hometown?

Senator Fred Thompson (R-TN)[60]

Transparency is wonderful. But we do not ask the Pentagon to educate the American public on the environmental costs of war, or the Environmental Protection Agency to preach on the benefits to the drug war of defoliating Latin America. Likewise, the SEC's role is not to inform Americans about the putative social, environmental, security, health, and other nonpecuniary costs and benefits that may attach to the activities of foreign companies.

Does this mean that Americans should not, or will not, be informed about the activities of foreign companies? Hardly. Members of Congress, the AFL-CIO, the Casey Institute, newspaper columnists, and the like all did their part to ensure widespread publicity for the debate over PetroChina's business. Forcing the SEC to put a government health warning on corporate disclosure statements, which are generally read only by professional analysts, would not have lent any more transparency to the issue; on the contrary, it would have obfuscated it by sending a deliberately muddy message about the U.S. government's true intentions.

But Don't Capital Markets Sanctions Have Symbolic Value?

According to the Casey Institute, "Irrespective of whether a foreign company or government incurs a significant financial penalty upon implementation of capital markets sanctions, there will likely be occasions when principled U.S. leadership requires action in our markets."[61] But leadership requires followers. And if America doesn't attract any—and for such sanctions, it never has—then the symbolism is one of abject impotence.

Then Why Capital Markets Sanctions?

Supporters of capital markets sanctions see them as much more than a tactic in a battle to achieve certain foreign policy ends. Whether on the right or the left, they tend to see capital market institutions such as the NYSE as the centerpiece of an amoral, international "neo-liberal regime" which undermines national interests and "traditional" social orders.[62] They mirror the right and left wings of the antiglobalization movement, which accord almost mythic political powers to the three Bretton Woods institutions—the IMF, the World Bank, and the WTO. This accounts for much of the naive triumphalism which surrounds the epic sanction tales of Gazprom and PetroChina—rank failures in terms of achieving foreign policy aims, but heroic in the fight itself.

Rarely has so powerful a force been harnessed by so many interests with such passion to so little positive effect. Yet unless the failure of capital markets sanctions as a foreign policy tool becomes far more widely understood, their political seductiveness is such that this no-cost, feel-good diplomatic toy gun will be wielded with ever greater frequency, undermining both the credibility of America's foreign policy as well as the attractiveness of its capital markets.

OF CURRENCIES AND CRISES

5

THE SECURITY DIMENSIONS
OF CURRENCY CRISES

Sometimes when we think of economics, we think we're only dealing with
economics. The background to all the Bretton Woods agreements,
however, was war and peace, and when people don't think in those terms,
I think they're making a major mistake.

—Rep. Jim Leach (R-IA)

The Rise of Geoeconomics

In 1972, President Nixon, upon hearing that the Fed chairman was
concerned about speculation against the Italian lira, responded, "Well, I don't
give a **** about the lira." Today, if an American president is warned about
possible speculation against the Thai baht, he is far more likely to give one.

The LDC debt crisis of the 1980s, as we discussed in chapter 2, galva-
nized economic policymakers in the United States, who were determined
to ensure that the American banking system would not be destabilized by
risky lending abroad. Despite the problems we identified with the capital
standards regime that became the centerpiece of this strategy, the heightened focus on risk management among bank management, investors, and
the financial press clearly began paying dividends in the 1990s, as debt
crises hit Latin America, Asia, and Russia with the U.S. banking sector
remaining relatively robust throughout.[1]

What U.S. policymakers were not prepared for, however, was the
geopolitical impact of foreign financial crises. It turns out that it wasn't
just the economy, stupid. Financial crises were increasingly figuring into
State Department, Pentagon, and National Security Council foreign policy concerns relating to matters such as political instability, defense
cooperation, nuclear proliferation, drug trafficking, transnational organized crime, and terrorism. By the late 1990s, financial crises around the
globe had become sufficiently frequent, widespread, and severe that they

had made their way into American presidential State of the Union addresses. In his January 1998 address, President Clinton talked about the crisis in Asia and emphasized the connection between economic stability abroad and American national security.[2]

Yet whereas the economic effects of financial crises in Asia, Russia, and Latin America have been subjected to much official quantification and commensurate lamentation, shockingly little has been written about how they actually relate to U.S. foreign policy and national security concerns. Former Secretary of State Henry Kissinger dedicates nearly an entire chapter to the Asia crisis in a recent book, *Does America Need a Foreign Policy?*, while observing a demure silence as to its actual *relevance* to American foreign policy.

In this chapter we discuss the U.S. national security issues emerging from the foreign financial crises of the past eight years. The point we emphasize is not that every consequence of the crises was unfavorable to U.S. security interests, but rather that the crises resulted in rapid and haphazard shifts in a security balance that was both input into and a target of Washington's long-term planning.

Chapter 6 will then focus on identifying the underlying economic causes of financial crises. Chapters 5 and 6 together set the stage for chapter 7, in which we discuss how U.S. foreign policy should adapt to global capital flows, given what we have learned about the causes and effects of foreign financial crises.

Asia

The massive currency devaluations that swept through the East Asian economies in 1997 cemented in policymakers' minds the firm belief that financial crises could be contagious. Such contagion is not just about economics. Or psychology. It is about politics.

Doubts over the ability of one country to meet its foreign currency obligations can quickly trigger not only doubts about the ability of other countries to pay, but also concerns about their governments taking precautionary measures, such as imposing capital controls, to bar the way out. Rational investors do not stand by waiting to parse official policy statements across potentially vulnerable countries—if someone yells "fire" in a bank anywhere in the neighborhood, they all rush for the exits. Financial collapse is the result. Routinely, the sellers are then fingered as financial arsonists, using dollars as their torches, and the blame redounds to the torch makers in Washington.

No two Asian countries hit by the crisis had precisely the same symptoms. Yet there were a number of symptoms prevalent to a greater or lesser degree across the region:

- currencies pegged closely to a rising dollar, damaging export competitiveness and foreign-exchange earnings;
- banks and businesses borrowing heavily in dollars short-term to invest longer-term locally or to speculate in real estate;
- politically directed credit allocation to unsound enterprises;
- poor or nonexistent supervision of bank lending practices and balance sheets;
- highly indebted large local enterprises with political connections, presaging ruinous bailouts in the event of a downturn.

With all these warning signs of overvalued currencies, was there not sufficient time for countries to take corrective action before mass selling of their currencies began? Certainly there was—in the same sense that there was sufficient time for American investors and businesses to take corrective action before the Nasdaq 100 index reached heights in 2000 which are now seen as being gross and obvious overvaluations. In both cases, however, there was optimism that great expectations could be indefinitely self-fulfilling—that is, that high borrowing and investment could be justified on the basis that historically exceptional recent growth rates could continue indefinitely.

Yet the suddenness and virulence of the currency collapses can be explained by a feature not present in the U.S. stock market: a promise by governments to use policy instruments and foreign exchange reserves to sustain the value of their currencies against the dollar, come what may.[3] This policy not only had the *effect* of encouraging local banks and businesses to behave as if devaluation were not a possibility, but was clearly its *intent*. The idea was that economic activity would be more robust the more borrowers and lenders could be persuaded to behave as if local currency earnings could be depended on to satisfy dollar debts. This strategy can perpetuate an overvalued currency for years on end, so long as investors believe the government is able, willing, or perhaps crazy enough to spend its dollar reserves, or jack up interest rates, to ward off sellers. But sellers will pounce with vehemence once they sense that a will or a way is lacking.

When it finally hit, the Asia crisis caused tremendous damage to livelihoods across the region. Currency values plummeted, banks and businesses collapsed, and an estimated 22 million people were pushed into poverty.[4] In Thailand, where the crisis started, unemployment rose from 0.9 percent in 1997 to 5.3 percent in 1998, and measures of poverty rose significantly. Household expenditure on health care declined by 40 percent from 1996 levels, with government unable to provide a buffer: the state's HIV/AIDS control budget, for example, was cut by a third in real terms.[5] But the hardest hit country was Indonesia, which at one point saw its currency, the rupiah, fall to a mere 15 percent of its pre-crisis value. The country's 13.8 percent GDP decline in 1998 was comparable to the total decline over the worst of the Depression years (1929–32) in the United Kingdom.[6]

The Asia crisis also produced some significant security and diplomatic headaches for the United States. In particular, the crisis resulted directly in regional political instability, including changes in government in Thailand, South Korea, and Indonesia; a dramatic rise in official anti-American public rhetoric; a precipitous falloff in regional defense commitments by key allies; a rise in transnational crime; a resurgence in interethnic conflict; and the growth of radical, anti-democratic Islamic movements, some openly advocating and engaging in terrorism. We examine these central political dimensions of the crisis below.

Anti-Americanism

Southeast Asian leaders noted the concern and generosity Washington showered upon Russia as it struggled with economic reforms and bristled at what they saw as a callous and indifferent approach as economic shockwaves spread across their region.[7] Conditions imposed by the IMF on financial assistance were seen as a cynical, opportunistic attempt by Washington to exploit the crisis on behalf of American banks and contractors seeking easier access in Asian markets. Washington's resistance to the creation of an Asian Monetary Fund was further seen as a means of ensuring that it could continue to meddle in Asian economic affairs with no regard for political and social effects. Such diverse regional voices as Malaysian Prime Minister Mahathir Mohamad and former Japanese Vice Minister Eisuke Sakakibara countered American charges that "crony capitalism" had undermined Asian economies with accusations that rapacious American hedge funds and other currency speculators were the true source of the havoc, widening a debate over how to address a financial crisis into a clash of cultural values over the social foundations of a market economy.

The sharp rise in Korean anti-American passions was particularly unnerving in Washington, as 36,000 American troops were stationed near the border with North Korea at a time of tense negotiations over the North's nuclear weapons program. Washington backed a record $57 billion IMF rescue package, described as "the financial equivalent of the Powell Doctrine," or the application of decisive and overwhelming force.[8] Yet as that package was announced on December 3, 1997, many South Koreans reacted in anger. The governing Grand National Party accused the IMF of "acting as if it is an economic conqueror," while the opposition National Congress for New Politics Party said that December 3rd would be remembered as "national economic humiliation day." Newspapers lamented Korea's loss of "economic sovereignty," using the term "economic trusteeship" to link the IMF package with the U.S., Soviet, British, and Chinese trusteeship of Korea in the aftermath of World War II, and accused the United States of exploiting the crisis to further its own commercial interests in the country. A major reform such as the dramatic raising of the ceiling on foreign ownership of Korean stocks to 50 percent would be highly emotive and controversial under normal circumstances, whereas the IMF gave the Korean government a mere 12 days to make it effective.[9] And, in the words of the *Korea Times*, "Everybody knows the IMF is run by the U.S."[10]

It was widely believed in Korea that the country could have avoided going to the hated IMF if Japan had provided $20 billion in emergency loans. Yet the Clinton administration opposed bilateral support from

Japan and urged Korea to deal with the IMF, seen in Korea as nothing more than a megaphone for the U.S. Treasury. Although Korean government officials were particularly bitter about their humiliation at the hands of the American government, they generally perceived themselves as being a buffer between the United States and an excitable Korean public. "If the U.S. government's negative role in the IMF negotiations becomes widely known to the public," explained a Ministry of Finance and Economy official, "anti-American sentiment could explode out of control in Korea."[11] Here was yet another wild card in U.S. policy planning for the region.

Defense

> The financial crisis which has rocked the region over the course of the past ten months has broad ramifications for U.S. security policy. The U.S. presence in Asia over the past half century provided a stable foundation on which the nations of the region achieved unprecedented economic progress. But just as peace and stability enabled economic progress, so too did economic progress reinforce peace and stability. The two, in fact, are intimately linked. And thus in the face of an economic crisis which is profoundly affecting the region, the progress that has been made on the security front can no longer be taken for granted.
>
> —Stanley Roth, U.S. Assistant Secretary of State for East Asian and Pacific Affairs, 1998[12]

> The United States views the Asian financial crisis as a core security concern.
>
> —Pentagon report, 1998[13]

The Asian financial crisis had a significant, direct effect on the security posture of every government in the region, creating a diplomatic as well as economic challenge for the Clinton administration—one that could easily have escalated into a military challenge had the crisis emerged in a less favorable regional political climate.

The crisis led directly to a worrisome falloff in defense capabilities among U.S. allies in the region and a relative strengthening in the ability of China and North Korea to pursue offensive postures antithetical to U.S. interests. As one analyst summarized it, "This crisis will significantly reduce readiness, defense spending, all forms of engagements with the Untied States, exercises of all sorts, weapons procurements, and international military cooperation across the board."[14]

Indonesia, Malaysia, Thailand, and the Philippines cut defense expenditures dramatically after 1996. Their combined expenditure bottomed out in 1999 at 76 percent of 1996 levels, in real terms, and did not surpass 1992 levels again until 2002.[15] Philippines President Joseph Estrada announced that his government could no longer afford to modernize and reform its armed forces and would have to rely on the United States for defense. Planned U.S. arms purchases by Asian allies, most notably F-18 and AWACS orders from Thailand, were canceled or scaled back. The Thai government, unhappy with Washington's initial response to the crisis, also informed U.S. Defense Secretary William Cohen that the United States could no longer count on the automatic use of Thai air and naval bases for transit to the Persian Gulf or Northeast Asia.[16]

Military resources were, furthermore, diverted to missions which increased regional frictions, such as Malaysia's use of its navy and air force to turn back Indonesian refugees fleeing economic turmoil in Indonesia. Within Indonesia, the army was called on to control violent outbursts directed against the Chinese merchant class.

The traditional defense posture in Southeast Asia has been predicated on the belief that China was a rising power dissatisfied with the territorial status quo, from Taiwan to the South China Sea islands. While the regional financial crisis decimated financing of this posture, China continued to spend prodigiously on its naval, air force, and strategic missile force capability, raising defense spending by nearly 13 percent in 1998. This led to concerns among American defense analysts that China could become more aggressive over time in pursuing sovereignty claims, particularly over the Spratly Islands, which would cause direct conflict with Brunei, Malaysia, the Philippines, Taiwan, and Vietnam.[17] Given China's growing ability to deter the United States from regional military intervention—demonstrated by her 1999 test-firing of the Dongfeng 31 missile, which has the capability to strike the American west coast—there is growing concern that the maritime members of the Association of Southeast Asian Nations (ASEAN) in particular will ultimately feel compelled to acquiesce to Chinese military and political control over the South China Sea.[18]

In Northeast Asia, the financial crisis raised concerns of renewed hostilities in the Korean Peninsula. North Korea's unexpected test-firing of its Taepodong 1 missile over Japan in August 1998, which alarmed both South Korea and Japan, has been interpreted as the North resorting to provocative measures to exploit economic and political uncertainty in the region.[19] Meanwhile, the public backlash against the United States and IMF in South Korea raised doubts about the long-term political sustainability of U.S. troop stationing in the country.

Not every change in the regional security constellation after the financial crisis was necessarily damaging to U.S. interests. The Philippines, for example, has sought to counter the rise of China as a regional power by more closely aligning its military with that of the United States and ASEAN partners South Korea, Malaysia, and Vietnam.[20] South Korea followed provocations by the North with its first joint naval exercise with Japan in August 1999. Regional cohesion among American allies has thus shown signs of improvement. This is a fortuitous development, to be sure, but it is like a tornado pulling a stuck car out of the mud: no one is thankful for the tornado, and they can only hope that the car has a safe landing.

Transnational Crime

In the wake of the financial crisis, Thailand, the Philippines, and Indonesia in particular experienced marked rises in transnational crime, including people-smuggling and other forms of illegal entry, drug production and trafficking (Thailand), and maritime piracy (Thailand and the Philippines). These problems were exacerbated by cuts in law enforcement (Thailand and Indonesia) and diversion of law enforcement to maintaining public order (Indonesia),[21] as well as by a steep decline in maritime patrolling (Indonesia's naval budget was cut by two-thirds). Deaths from piracy in the South China Sea rose sharply in 1998, and maritime officials fear an environmental disaster or major terrorist incident in the Malacca straits unless patrolling resources are restored.[22]

Interethnic Conflict

Ethnic Chinese inhabitants of Indonesia, while representing a mere 3.5 percent of the population, control nearly 75 percent of the country's assets and nine of the top 10 business groups. In the wake of the financial crisis and the rapid rise in food, fuel, and other staple prices, their homes, businesses, and churches were targeted for looting and arson.[23] Washington has long been concerned that conflict between ethnic Chinese and the ethnic (largely Muslim) majorities in Indonesia and Malaysia could lead to rising tensions with China, which maintained a policy until the late 1980s of regarding ethnic Chinese in Southeast Asia as Chinese citizens.[24] Heightened refugee flows, particularly from Indonesia to Malaysia and Myanmar to Thailand, increased regional political tensions, although maturation of ASEAN political cooperation helped to keep them within manageable limits.[25] The crisis also fueled secessionist sentiments and huge demonstrations in the Indonesian state of Aceh, the primary source of Indonesia's refugee outflows, and catalyzed the independence movement in East Timor, raising doubts about the long-term territorial integrity of the Indonesian archipelago.[26]

Terrorism

Socio-economic factors have fostered further support for radical Islamic groups in the region. . . . The Asian financial crisis since 1997 has also put pressures on regional governments and spending on crucial areas such as education has been restricted. This has increased the attraction of religious schools. Furthermore, well-funded Islamic radical movements have been able to offer financial support both to adherents and their families (for example in the event of death in combat). This has had considerable appeal to those in outlying and economically disadvantaged areas.

—Australian Parliamentary Report[27]

The Southeast Asian terrorist network Jemaah Islamiyah (JI), led by Indonesian nationals, was created in Malaysia around 1995. JI is widely believed to have been behind the October 2002 terrorist bombing in Bali that killed over 200 mostly foreign tourists. Supported by Al Qaeda with money, training, and weapons, JI benefited significantly from the economic and political turmoil surrounding the Asian financial crisis. One of its founders, the Indonesian cleric Riduan Isamuddin, alias Hambali, considered the region's top Al Qaeda agent, began organizing militant cells in earnest in 1997 and 1998, during the heart of the crisis.[28]

Central to the rise of JI were five factors related to the crisis:

- the collapse of employment opportunities across the region;
- an upsurge of economic grievance, fundamentalism, political activism, and militancy among the region's 300 million Muslims;[29]
- the shift in enrollment from under-resourced state-run schools to *pesantrens,* or Islamic boarding schools teaching anti-Western thought; [30]
- national political crises in Indonesia, Malaysia, and the Philippines, creating power vacuums ripe for exploitation by the well-funded extremists, whom weak governments (such as Megawati's post-Suharto administration in Indonesia) were loath to challenge for fear of backlash; and
- the failure of local authorities to monitor the increasingly sophisticated, interconnected terror cells.[31]

The nature of the relationship between economic conditions and terrorism is a hotly debated one. Deprivation or an absence of opportunity, however, need not *cause* terrorism in order for them to play a significant role in abetting its growth. In the case of Southeast Asia, economic collapse clearly created a credibility chasm among the ruling political elites that increased the appeal of radical alternatives among those most harshly affected.

Russia

The proximate cause of the August 1998 collapse of the Russian currency, the ruble, was the Russian government's inability to service its massive short-term debt. Nearly a quarter of its expenditures in the early months of 1998 were for interest payments, and the government was borrowing an additional $1 billion each week to replace the maturing bonds, known as GKOs, a third of which were owned by foreigners. Interest rates on GKOs soared from 25 percent in April to 150 percent in August, finally forcing the Russian government to restructure its debt and devalue the ruble after the IMF balked at further aid, $22 billion having been disbursed since 1992.

The financial crisis significantly exacerbated two interrelated security problems for the United States. The first was a dramatic expansion of

Russian organized crime, which has been linked to money laundering, kidnapping, armed robbery, arson, and weapons proliferation around the world. The second was a decline in the ability of the Russian government to finance and control the safeguarding and destruction of its weapons of mass destruction stockpile, and a corresponding rise in the risk that criminal groups would gain control of such weapons and try to sell them abroad.

Organized Crime

The Russian banking system, huge holders of GKOs and underwriters of exchange risk to foreign holders, collapsed with the government's default and devaluation. This effectively severed Moscow's financial links with and authority over the regions and pushed cash-starved firms and regional authorities deeper into an already corrupt system of informal exchange and barter. Organized crime syndicates moved into the power vacuum, establishing control over these arrangements and administering their own form of violent justice against those who crossed them. They further spread their influence through the Russian state security apparatus and expanded their operations into other countries, such as Poland, Hungary, Colombia, Brazil, Israel, and the United States. In 1999, Russian mob figures were discovered to have run a massive money-laundering operation through the Bank of New York, estimated to have involved up to $15 billion. A major American report on Russian organized crime called on the president to recognize it publicly as a "national security threat." [32]

Weapons Proliferation

Because desperate people do desperate things, we should pay attention to any region of the world where hunger and economic hopelessness are prevalent. But when desperate people have access to weapons of mass destruction, we must do more than pay attention. We must approach the problem with the same focus and seriousness of purpose with which we approached the Cold War.

—Senator Richard Lugar (R-IN)[33]

The international economic crisis that spread to Russia in 1998 has dramatically increased the risks of possible proliferation of weapons of mass destruction. . . . It is the Department's assessment that in their current economic crisis the elimination of excess missiles, bombers and SSBNs is not a high budget priority for the Russian government. We believe that

> rather than dismantling these systems, Moscow would most likely leave them untended. It is our fear that these systems pose a grave proliferation risk to the United States should they fall into the wrong hands.
>
> —former Assistant Secretary of Defense Edward L. Warner[34]

The aftermath of the collapse of the ruble left a perilous void in Russia's security arrangements for weapons and weapons material. In September 1998, an American team visiting the Kurchatov Institute in Moscow found 100 kilograms of highly enriched uranium—potentially enough for several nuclear bombs—wholly unguarded. The institute could no longer afford the $200 a month for a guard. At the Novaya Zemlya nuclear test site, soldiers charged with guarding the facilities killed a guard, took hostages, and tried to hijack an airplane before being disarmed by other defense forces. In November, it was reported that guards had left their posts at several nuclear facilities in order to forage for food. Others were reluctant to patrol perimeter areas for lack of warm clothes. At some facilities, alarms, surveillance cameras, portal monitors, and other security devices were inoperative owing to lack of electricity, which was cut off after nonpayment of bills. Workers at one of Russia's premier nuclear weapons laboratories, Chelyabinsk-70, staged a strike, complaining of lack of food, medical care, and money to pay for children's clothes and education.[35] In December, the chief of the Russian Federal Security Service in the Chelyabinsk region reported that employees at one of the facilities had been caught trying to steal 18.5 kilograms of weapons-usable nuclear material.[36] Many such facilities had lost funds in collapsed Russian banks.

U.S. experts estimated that 650 tons of highly enriched uranium and plutonium stored outside nuclear weapons had been left at risk of theft and diversion specifically because of the financial crisis.[37] Scattered across 11 time zones, in civilian scientific centers and military research institutes, this material was highly vulnerable. Numerous incidents relating to theft and trafficking of Russian nuclear or radioactive materials have been documented since the crisis.[38] Criminal organizations as well as members of the armed forces, who have suffered a severe decline in pay and status, are heavily involved in all aspects of the arms market.[39] It is impossible to estimate how much deadly material has now entered into the international marketplace, but the matter remains one of deep concern to American national security experts.

Latin America

The period since the presidency of Bush père in the late 1980s has been notable for the unprecedented consistent, constructive engagement that has marked American policy toward Latin America. This approach was reciprocated by a remarkable surge in pro-American sentiment in the region—at least through the first half of the 1990s. The second half brought an end to this honeymoon.

The late 1990s witnessed a severe economic downturn in Latin America that culminated in financial collapse in Argentina and crisis in Brazil. Economic growth slowed from an annual average of 4.2 percent in the first half of the decade to only 2 percent in the second, turning negative after 2000. Unemployment in 2003 reached its highest level in over two decades, and poverty has been on the rise. Private savings have flown out of the region, such holdings having reached about $700 billion.[40] Economic troubles were accompanied by a revival of traditionally hostile attitudes toward private enterprise and market forces. The political effect was unsurprising: the ouster of all the region's political leaders who backed Washington's economic reform agenda and the rise of populist politicians who, to varying degrees, have halted or reversed their policies.

From the Potomac perspective, U.S. foreign policy is no less benign and supportive toward Latin America now than it was in the late 1980s. But south of the border, economic troubles are seen as being intimately connected with U.S. foreign policy. In particular, the fact that a huge U.S. bailout package like the one granted to Mexico in the wake of its 1994 peso crisis was conspicuously absent in the more recent cases of Argentina and Brazil is seen in the region as having nothing to do with contagion fears having been greater in 1994, but with the United States having of late written off the region as a political irrelevance.

Nowhere is this feeling more powerful than in Argentina. The *Washington Post* described the transformation in public sentiment toward the United States over the past decade as follows:

In the 1990s, the Argentine economy ignited under U.S.-backed free-market reforms and "American chic" became cool in this pulsing metropolis [Buenos Aires]. As substantial foreign investment reversed decades of strained relations between Buenos Aires and Washington, nightclubs painted their dance floors in the Stars and Stripes. English words such as "shopping" and "fashion" became part of the local lexicon. Movie theaters adopted the alien custom of selling popcorn to please customers desperate to do things the American way.

But as Latin America's third-largest economy suffers its worst collapse since the Great Depression, anti-American sentiment is on the rise. Banks, McDonald's restaurants and other American symbols have been attacked in Buenos Aires. Argentine newsmagazines and politicians are even alleging a U.S. plot to destroy the economy.[41]

IMF conditionality on loans to ward off or mitigate currency collapse and default was widely seen in Argentina as U.S.-inspired blackmail to support American commercial interests. For example, IMF demands for the repeal of Argentine laws supporting debt-laden domestic enterprises were popularly interpreted as a cynical plot to help American creditors take over major Argentine media and farming conglomerates. Leading newsmagazines published cover stories on speculation that Washington was seeking to deepen Argentina's crisis so as to topple the president, further undermine the peso, and assist American companies in snatching up the best farmland in Pampas. Opposition politicians railed against U.S. interests they alleged to be exploiting the crisis to buy up more of the country.[42]

This feeling of betrayal and abandonment by Washington is echoed throughout Latin America. According to a *New York Times* report from Brazil, "The United States is . . . paying for what is seen here as indifference to an economic crisis that swept this region a few years after its leaders took American advice to open their markets and embrace globalization. . . . 'When you had the promise of globalization and free markets, people warmed up to the idea that the American dream of prosperity might come to us,' said Felipe Noguera, a poll taker and political analyst here. But now public opinion throughout the region has again become, he said, 'like a growling dog.'"[43]

Democratization

The region is falling into financial crises that are sapping confidence in the value of democracy.
—former Uruguayan President Julio María Sanguinetti[44]

A 2002 UN Development Program survey found, disturbingly, that a majority of Latin Americans would prefer authoritarian rule if it would improve their lives economically. Democracy, a report based on the survey concluded, was suffering a "profound crisis of confidence" throughout the region.[45] Essential to ensuring that Latin Americans do not come indelibly to associate democratization with impoverishment is to protect their savings from the ravishment of further bouts of inflation and devaluation. Failure to do so will also threaten to drag U.S.–Latin America relations back into the dark ages of the 1970s and 1980s, when Washington's diplomatic choices were frequently limited to tolerating anti-American leftist regimes or supporting authoritarian right wing ones.

Drugs and Money Laundering

Venezuela is a major drug money laundering center owing to its proximity to Colombia and the relative development of its financial markets. Money laundering in Venezuela is closely linked to cocaine trafficking by Colombian organizations. Whereas the narcotics proceeds are primarily owned by Colombian or other third-country nationals, the money laundering networks are generally run by Venezuelans. Laundering transactions usually involves the exchange of dollars in cash or in monetary instruments such as postal money orders for Colombian pesos or Venezuelan bolivares.

Venezuelan government exchange controls were imposed in 1994 to staunch the outflow of flight capital occurring during their financial crisis. While unintended, these policies helped stimulate the growth of a large illegal parallel exchange market, which created new opportunities for money launderers to exploit.[46] Financial crises, money laundering, and the drug trade are all, therefore, symbiotically linked, creating security, law enforcement, and public health concerns for the United States.

Terrorism

The Tri-Border Area (TBA) of Argentina, Brazil, and Paraguay has long been a haven for criminal groups active in drug trafficking, arms trafficking, sex trafficking, money laundering, and terrorism. Lax immigration controls and official corruption in the TBA have eased the entry of Islamic extremists from outside the region, many using purchased false passports and visas.[47] Islamic extremist organizations such as Hezbollah, Hamas, and Al Qaeda are all believed to operate in the TBA. Osama bin Laden himself was said to have been in the area in 1995,[48] and by October 2001 the FBI had reportedly found evidence identifying the TBA as Al Qaeda's center of operations for Latin America.[49]

Argentina has been central to U.S. counterterrorism in Latin America, being the most cooperative country in the TBA in sharing intelligence with U.S. authorities.[50] Yet, according to a U.S. defense intelligence officer, information flows from Argentina on terrorist activity in the region declined after the country's financial crisis led to a diversion of resources to containing domestic unrest.[51] In March 2002, defense analysts Harold Trinkunas and Jack Boureston described the effect of the financial crisis as follows:

> The crisis . . . has serious implications for Argentine and regional security. In the short term, the heavy strain placed on Argentine police forces by frequent riot control duty in major cities is likely to erode their capacity to deal with other threats to internal security. In particular, terrorist groups linked to Hamas and Hezbollah are strongly suspected of operating in the tri-border region where Argentina, Paraguay, and Brazil meet. These groups are thought to have carried out the bombing of the Israeli embassy in Buenos Aires in the 1990s. A weakened Argentine security presence in this already under-policed region at a time of local political turmoil may create new opportunities for these groups to prosper.[52]

In March 2003, U.S. Army General James T. Hill described the effect of the crisis before the House Armed Services Committee as follows:

In recent years, economic desperation and volatile social environments in the hemisphere have set the conditions for the proliferation of international terrorism, narcoterrorism, illegal drugs, and arms trafficking. This is the crux of my concern and responsibility. Unless and until Latin American and Caribbean governments can provide both security and stability and a reasonable opportunity for positive change in the lives of their citizens, these activities will continue to fester and grow and the foundations of democracy could crumble under the weight of these transnational threats.[53]

Given the proximity of these threats to America's borders, the importance of avoiding the emergence of the security vacuum described by General Hill is obvious.

The Next Step

The world of international finance has changed dramatically since President Nixon famously failed to give a **** about the lira. Since the 1980s, when dollars began moving into, and then out of, developing countries in great volumes and at great speeds, the nexus between the stability of national currencies and international relations has become an increasingly important and, at times, perilous one for the United States. Although not all postcrisis political effects have been antithetical to U.S. interests—democratization in Indonesia is certainly consistent with long-proclaimed U.S. goals for that region—most clearly were, and all took place in a chaotic environment which, in less benign circumstances, could have created security crises, rather than mere challenges, for the United States.

Understanding the causes of financial crises is the first step on the path to making their prevention and containment an effective part of American foreign policy. Our next chapter aims to take this step.

6

THE ECONOMICS OF FINANCIAL CRISES

It's the Currency, Stupid

Over the past two decades, financial crises have hit countries across Latin America and Asia, as well as countries just beyond the borders of western Europe—in particular, Russia and Turkey. Roubini and Setser conclude that "all crises are unique."[1] Indeed, no two crisis countries appear to make precisely the same errors or to face the same market reactions when appearing to follow the same policies. There is, however, one commonality that virtually defines the onset of crisis. Holders of the crisis country's currency begin selling it rapidly and in large amounts, almost invariably for dollars. "Crisis" is effectively shorthand for "currency crisis."

But why does a currency crisis occur? Here is where things get murky. We know that crisis countries and their creditors violate Polonius's stricture neither borrower nor lender to be, yet some countries borrow far more prodigiously than others while never experiencing a crisis. Richer countries and those with spotless debt repayment records (generally one and the same) can support a vastly larger debt burden without triggering creditor panic than poorer ones with numerous default episodes. Japan's debt-to-GDP ratio of about 140 percent is well over twice Argentina's at the time of its default in 2001 or Mexico's when it defaulted in 1982, yet it pays among the lowest real interest rates of all sovereign borrowers. Serial defaulters, on the other hand, can find themselves under market pressure with debt ratios as low as 20 percent.[2]

So how then does borrowing lead to a crisis?

Suppose a company in Argentina seeks a bank loan to finance a new factory. Suppose as well that the company decides to borrow the money in dollars rather than pesos, owing to the lower interest rate on dollar loans. Finally, suppose that the factory is expected to produce a predictable stream of sales revenue in pesos; enough at the current exchange rate to pay off the loan and leave the company with a net profit of 20 percent.

This arrangement works nicely for the company and for the bank, provided that the peso maintains its value or rises against the dollar. Should it fall, however, the company will find it more costly to pay back the dollar loan. Should it fall by more than 20 percent, the revenue from the factory will be insufficient to pay back the loan, and the company will have to find dollars elsewhere or default.

Imagine such a scenario extended across an entire national economy. Companies, households, and the government itself finance their local-currency activities with "cheap" dollars, fueling economic growth and rising living standards for as long as the local currency remains strong. But should it take a steep dive for any reason, the currency mismatch between the country's local-money assets and its dollar liabilities will result in widespread default, bankruptcy, inflation, and unemployment.

And this is if the country is lucky. If it is not lucky, we can add to the list such items as malnutrition, disease, lawlessness, violence, and political upheaval.

Almost every major national financial crisis over the past decade has had currency mismatch at its root.[3] As we shall see as well, such crises are brutally difficult to contain and resolve. No one—certainly not the IMF, the U.S. Treasury, or Wall Street seers—knows in any given case precisely what economic medicine or how much of it is needed in the midst of a crisis to persuade a country's citizens and its outside investors and creditors that it is in their interests to stop selling local currency. High interest rates may staunch the selling but may also push thousands of firms needing financing into bankruptcy. Keeping them low, however, may fuel the selling and thereby bankrupt the dollar borrowers as well as their lenders. This is why it is so vitally important to focus on preventative measures.

Anticipating Crises

Countries, like companies, have balance sheets. They have assets and liabilities. The assets include all sorts of valuable things that the government and its citizens own, like land, buildings, and loans outstanding to others. The liabilities are the mirror image, valuable things which are owed as a debt to others.

One critical reason for the vast disparities in the way creditors react to different national balance sheets is that countries do not go "bankrupt" in the way companies do. Companies legally go bankrupt when their assets are insufficient to cover their liabilities. National insolvency, however, is ultimately discretionary. In principle, countries can always sell a few lakes or mountains to meet their debts. It is in this sense that Walter Wriston's infamous quip during the Latin American crisis of the early 1980s—"countries don't go bankrupt"—is technically correct. Governments weigh the costs of default, such as the damage it will do to their financial systems and their future cost of borrowing, against the obvious benefits of shedding their existing debts. These costs and benefits vary dramatically across countries. The fact that national insolvency is ultimately discretionary, however, means that crises can never be predicted on the basis of simple balance sheet ratios.

The degree to which a country is at risk of experiencing a currency crisis is partly related to the way in which both sides of the balance sheet—the assets and the liabilities, or the country's "net worth"—will be affected by a change in the exchange rate. The second element is the degree to which its "net income," its revenue and expenditure flows, will be affected by a change in the exchange rate.[4] All else being equal, a country with greater foreign assets (such as dollar reserves) or export revenues can support a higher level of foreign borrowing than one with fewer foreign assets or lower export earnings.

Who owes what debt to whom is of great importance in gauging whether a country is at risk of crisis. The debt can be internal (held within the country) or external (held by foreigners). The debt can be public sector (obligations of the government) or private sector (obligations of companies or the citizens themselves). The debt can be shorter-term or longer-term. Finally, the debt can be denominated in the national currency or in a foreign currency (or currencies). Whereas the source of the debt problem has differed significantly across crisis countries, the way the debt problem ultimately manifested itself in crisis did not. At the end of a chain of reactions, there was always massive selling of the domestic currency for dollars.

In Mexico and Russia, both of which had pegged their currencies to the dollar, public debt was a major culprit, but in very different ways. In Mexico, the stock of dollar-linked "tesebono" debt grew by ten times between February and December 1994, yielding a public-sector debt that exceeded the rapidly falling stock of foreign reserves by about $10 billion. Unlike Mexico, the Russian government sold its GKO debt to foreigners in domestic currency, rubles. However, the foreigners—who had increased their GKO holdings from 17 percent of the total in late 1996 to 33 percent by the summer of 1998—hedged the exchange risk by buying forward contracts, guaranteeing the future dollar-value of the bonds' ruble proceeds, from Russian banks, which had grossly insufficient dollar assets to make good on those contracts in the event of a ruble collapse. This was the fatal source of currency mismatch in the Russian economy, which both fueled mass selling of the ruble and undermined the entire banking system when the Russian government defaulted on its ballooning ruble debt.

In Asia, unlike Mexico or Russia, it was private rather than public debt that was the source of the problem. In Korea, borrowing by domestic banks from foreign banks (generally in dollars) nearly doubled as a percentage of their lending to domestic firms, from 25 to 46 percent, between 1995 and 1997.[5] In Thailand, which ran a government budget surplus in 1995 and 1996, nonbank finance companies accounting for about 20 percent of domestic credit were chief culprits, borrowing dollars short-term abroad and lending baht to real estate and stock market speculators, among others, at home. When the economy began to tank in 1996, domestic nonperforming loans rocketed, the current-account deficit soared, and foreign speculators attacked the baht, which had become transparently overvalued against a dollar-heavy currency basket to which it was pegged. In Indonesia, foreign liabilities of the largest firms, those listed on the stock market, were a major source of vulnerability: 95 percent of such liabilities were unhedged in the agriculture, mining, real estate, construction, and financial sectors.[6]

Whodunnit?

It is a convenient but inaccurate shorthand to lay the blame for these financial crises at the door of currency-market volatility. But measures of currency-market volatility are, in fact, poor indicators of financial crises.[7] Furthermore, the favored snake oil of the "antiglobalization" movement, a "Tobin tax" on currency transactions, would have had precisely no effect in preventing the Asia crisis. These countries were not laid low by day-trading. Their foreign currency liabilities were built up over years, while the financial sector reforms necessary to manage them safely were never undertaken. These liabilities accrued despite the fact that transaction spreads in those markets were generally on the order of 50 times higher than a 0.1 percent Tobin Tax, which was itself supposed to deter capital flows. And once the prospect of 30 percent devaluations became real, an exit tax this minuscule was hardly going to be a deterrent to capital flight.

Similarly, it is no more helpful to point the finger at "distortions" or "imperfections" in global financial markets than it is to blame oxygen for forest fires. Some have pointed to the inability of all but a handful of countries to borrow abroad in their own currency as one such imperfection.[8] Yet whereas a compelling argument can be made to the effect that investors hold a much smaller number of currencies in their global portfolio than they would in the absence of transactions costs and network externalities, both of these "imperfections" are endemic to financial markets, and nothing is to be gained from pointing out that countries are less well served by real-world global markets which exclude their currencies than they are by idealized versions which assume that transaction costs and network externalities do not exist.[9]

In the final analysis, it is currency mismatch created by a country's borrowing behavior that determines its vulnerability to crisis. Examining the volume of short-term unhedged foreign currency debt, Furman and Stiglitz (1998) conclude that "the ability of this variable, by itself, to predict the [Asian] crises of 1997 is remarkable." Precisely how risky such debt is depends on whether there are sufficient foreign assets to cover the liabilities. The ratio of short-term external debt to foreign reserves is a fairly reliable indicator: a ratio below one is generally a sign of danger.[10]

Foreign Assistance

The IMF and the U.S. Treasury, in particular, have frequently provided multibillion-dollar loan packages to help countries avoid financial crisis. While there have been a few notable successes, such as Mexico in 1995, the general track record is poor. Why?

Borrowing more dollars cannot improve a country's balance sheet. The inflow adds to the country's assets only at the cost of adding new senior debt to its liabilities. If the country's balance sheet is suffering from a currency mismatch across the combined private and public sectors, existing creditors will conclude that such support can only temporarily postpone default. Currency mismatch is a fundamental source of solvency risk, and solvency risk cannot be reduced with more loans.

Only where the country is suffering from a maturity mismatch, or liquidity risk, can outside loans be effective. Distinguishing liquidity risk from solvency risk is more art than science, unfortunately, as only confidence stands between the first becoming the second. Creditors must be confident that the country will have future dollar assets sufficient to cover existing dollar debts as well as any newly acquired emergency debt. In other words, they must believe that new loans can bridge the time gap between the implementation and ultimate success of measures to earn more dollars or to staunch their outflow.[11]

In the collapse phase of a crisis, the national currency plummets. If not stemmed, the effect is to trigger shock waves of bankruptcy through the economy, as firms with dollar liabilities default, bringing their banks down with them. Whatever lessons the IMF may have learned from past crises about what *not* to do in the midst of a currency meltdown, neither they nor their harshest critics have yet discovered an alternative to higher interest rates as an emergency stabilization device. Damn it as "orthodoxy" or the "Washington Consensus," but you might as well be raging against the laws of physics. This is about as close to an economic truism as you can get: when a central bank spews credit at unchanged interest rates in the midst of a currency collapse, borrowers converge like vultures at the hunt while lenders run for cover. Not to raise rates is often simply to pour fuel on the fire.

If this seems too harsh a road to take, the only reliable solution is the one offered by the proverbial Irishman asked for the road to Dublin. Best not to start from here.

Dealing with Currency Mismatch at Home

Goldstein and Turner (2004), in a magisterial analysis of currency mismatch, recommend an eight-point approach to mitigating the problems created by it: (1) a "managed floating" exchange rate policy, (2) inflation targeting, (3) better bank monitoring of currency mismatches, (4) better bank supervisor monitoring of bank monitoring of currency mismatches, (5) more aggressive and timely supervisor interventions and bank closures, (6) better IMF data on currency mismatches, (7) better government review of debt and reserve management policies, and (8) higher government priority to "developing" domestic bond markets and "encouraging" the availability of hedging instruments.

While their analysis of the problem of currency mismatch is a scholarly tour de force, we see three problems with their response. The first is a narrow one: the call for managed floating will at some point conflict with the call for inflation targeting. It is not possible simultaneously to target the inflation rate *and* the exchange rate.[12] The second is a broad one: the list is far more hortative than instructive. It is always sensible to call for better data, prudence, vigilance, and encouragement, but there is nothing new in these pleas, and interested readers will have to look elsewhere for a how-to manual. The third is that critical weaknesses in the banking sector are endemic to financially dollarized economies with managed exchange rates. It is axiomatic that after any national currency crisis macroeconomists will damn the "weak" banking sector and its regulator and argue that both should have been "strengthened" before allowing capital flows. But no country with low levels of short-term external debt relative to reserves was hit in the Asia crisis, even those with high levels of corruption and weak banking systems. The issue is currency mismatch itself.

Consider the situation of two banking systems, one American and one Argentine, the latter operating under a fixed exchange rate or currency board. The American banks are dollar-based operations with exposure in nontradable currencies, owing to activities abroad. The Argentine banks are (nontradable) peso-based operations with massive exposure in dollars, owing to a high level of domestic corporate demand for lower-interest dollar loans. The default rate on such dollar loans will be high should the peso be devalued before the loans come due, as the companies earn their revenues in pesos. Should the Argentine banks hedge, or be obliged to hedge, against this risk? The government regulating the banks can hardly wave red flags about unhedged currency risk while maintaining publicly that a peso is just a dollar with Argentine heroes on it. And imagine what would happen if the entire Argentine banking sector *did* hedge against loan losses by selling pesos in the forward market. The downward pressure on the peso would bring about the very devaluation and defaults they were so prudently hedging against in the first place. In short, a financially dollarized economy is so inherently dangerous that a weak banking sector becomes part and parcel of it.

Given the gravity of the past decade's financial crises, and Goldstein and Turner's justifiable conviction in fingering currency mismatch, it is natural to question whether their plan for addressing it is ultimately deck chair rotation on the *Titanic*. They do not, for example, call for elimination of the offending local currencies, instead granting them a stay of execution on the grounds that their death will hamper countercyclical interventions and require more economic "flexibility" than they feel these countries capable of.

But the historical record of activist central-bank economic-cycle smoothing in developing countries is atrocious. And the empirical evidence on discretionary fiscal policy links it strongly with macroeconomic *instability* and *lower growth*.[13] Most important, the assumption that governments can successfully reform monetary policy, banking supervision, debt management, and capital market structure while being unable to inject economic "flexibility" is wholly contradictory. Better to treat the problem than the symptoms, particularly when the symptoms are far more numerous and complex.

Who Needs Capital Flows?

It is taken for granted that capital should flow freely within countries, although even many free-market-oriented economists have strong reservations about the universal wisdom of accommodating unfettered (particularly short-term) capital flows across national borders. This is no doubt a reaction to the recurrence of major national and regional currency crises over the past two decades.

The theoretical case for capital flows is compelling to the point of being obvious. When capital can flow freely from where it is overabundant to where it is scarce, the return on savers' capital is maximized and its cost to growing companies is minimized. Norway, for example, was a huge importer of capital (as high as 14 percent of GDP) in the 1970s, allowing it to develop its oil reserves far more cheaply than it could have by relying on domestic savings. Singapore, on the other hand, was a mirror-image exporter of capital in the 1990s, allowing its citizens to achieve much higher returns on their savings than they could ever have achieved at home.[14] Free capital flows also allow financial risks to be pooled, and therefore lessened through diversification, and better allocated among those with different abilities to bear and manage them. When capital flows function in this manner, they are a major stimulant to economic growth and higher living standards.

Are high levels of capital inflows inherently dangerous? Not on their own. Between 1870 and 1890, Argentina imported capital equivalent to 18.7 percent of GDP, compared with barely over 2 percent in 1990–96, the years prior to a major currency crisis. Indeed, international capital flows for twelve major trading nations were roughly 60 percent higher as a percentage of GDP from 1870 to 1890 than they were in the 1990s.[15] There is proportionately less capital crossing borders today than there was a century ago.[16]

Consider too that capital today flows freely, instantaneously, and often massively within countries. During the 1990s tech boom, billions of dollars were raised in New York and invested in California. When the tech bubble finally burst with the dawning of the new millennium, both the California and New York economies were hit hard, as companies and their investors suffered the grim aftermath of irrational exuberance. Yet through the highs and the lows there were no capital account crises, no speculative currency attacks, no cessations of credit, no interest rate spikes, no bank runs, no IMF missions, no violent protests, and no political upheavals.

We know of no economist who questions the wisdom of free capital flows between the continental United States and the commonwealth of Puerto Rico; or dollarized Panama, Ecuador, and El Salvador, for that matter. While the evils of "hot money" rushing into and out of emerging markets are widely proclaimed, the condemnation is reserved exclusively for dollars sweeping through states whose governments restrict their use or refuse to use them in dealings with their citizens. In other words, it is not the movement of money between the rich and poor parts of the world that is damned, but the movement of dollars in and out of countries whose governments don't want their citizens to use them. The political presumption on the part of capital-flow critics is in favor of the governments, and therefore the solution is always to stop citizens from importing or exporting capital.

State Money

> So much of barbarism . . . still remains in the transactions of most civilized nations, that almost all independent countries choose to assert their nationality by having, to their own inconvenience and that of their neighbours, a peculiar currency of their own.
>
> —John Stuart Mill[17]

Being a country means having a sovereign currency. And therein lies the source of so much immiseration and international hostility that the only wonder is how it came to be seen so widely as a natural and immutable state of affairs.

It wasn't always such. The financially integrated world of the early twentieth century had gold as its foundation. Gold had unique credibility as a store of value, given its universal desirability, durability, and relatively stable supply. This last factor was critical to its success as a global monetary base. The supply of monetary gold was determined by the mechanical interaction of nonmonetary gold demand and mining production. This contrasts with the supply of today's fiat money, which can be expanded instantly at the whim of governments, without limits. The nondiscretionary nature of the monetary gold supply accounts for the universal trust that was vested in it. Gold thereby became the medium by which a commitment to international trade across much of the globe was successfully operationalized.

Given the enormous difficulties that periodic financial crises have, over the past two decades, posed for the integration of developing market economies into the vast, established trading network of the rich nations, it is critical to note that it was the universal commitment to gold that facilitated the massive transfer of long-term capital from Europe to the new world over the four decades prior to World War I.[18] Such a successful transfer from rich to poor has proven impossible, and at times highly destructive, in our age of autarkic national currencies. It is further important to note that short-term capital flows actually played a highly *stabilizing* role during the late nineteenth century, allowing rapid adjustment to balance-of-payment disturbances through interest-rate arbitrage. The cross-border flow of gold itself was peripheral to the adjustment mechanism.

This system slowly edged toward crisis in the run-up to World War I, however, as national monies became progressively less tethered to gold. A gold standard had evolved into a gold exchange standard, in which national monies came to substitute, as reserves, for gold itself. The onset of war led to a scramble to exchange currencies for the real thing, physical gold, thereby collapsing what had become "a massive pyramid of credit built upon a narrow base of gold."[19] A parallel effect can be witnessed today, based around the dollar rather than gold, each time foreign creditors begin to sense that debtor nations lack sufficient dollar reserves to meet all their international payment obligations.

In spite of its many properties that make it desirable as a monetary instrument, gold is not a nirvana money. No such thing exists outside the algebraic world of textbooks. The gold standard had some well-known flaws, deriving from shocks to gold supply and demand, that made the price level unpredictable in the short run. Supply uncertainty and volatility mean that gold cannot be a guarantor of world price stability. Furthermore, the powerful economic incentive to substitute interest-bearing assets and cheaper transaction surrogates for actual gold ultimately puts tremendous responsibility for maintaining confidence in the "pyramid of credit" on the predominant central bank. This role, which the Bank of England played in the nineteenth century, is played today by the U.S. Federal Reserve, and would be so with or without some form of gold exchange standard.

We are, then, left with a conundrum. Gold, for all its limitations, is the only successful foundation for global economic integration that humankind has yet discovered. Yet just as derivative instruments make investment and risk management far more efficient than they would be without them, but at the cost of periodic financial disasters based on underestimated leverage and faulty economic assumptions, paper (or completely dematerialized) currencies make it far more efficient to trade and invest globally, albeit at the cost of vastly more serious countrywide or even international financial disasters. Can we recreate the stability of the gold-era globalization while still taking the fullest advantage of capital-flow dematerialization?

We can, if we take to heart the lessons of gold's success. Gold represented a rock-solid convertibility *rule* which allowed policymakers no discretion to pursue new objectives, such as using inflation to increase seigniorage revenue or to reduce the value of debt obligations, that could undermine the confidence of goods and capital traders in the future value of monies linked to gold. And indeed, the vast improvement in monetary policy performance among the wealthy nations over the past two decades has been based on the substitution of rules for discretion in the operation of monetary policy. Central banks independent of political control, operating transparently under some form of inflation target, whether explicit or understood, have established the solid economic foundations upon which long-term investments, 30-year mortgages, and the like could take root.

The process of refashioning the world's monetary system on rules rather than political discretion has certainly not been a smooth or painless one. The interwar gold standard lasted only six years, from 1925 to 1931, largely because the political commitment to convertibility was not nearly as credible as under the prewar standard. Among the many flaws was mass substitution of currencies for gold as international reserves—similar conceptually to Argentina's substituting peso assets for dollars in its currency board in the prelude to its collapse in 2001.

The post–World War II Bretton Woods system was built far more on a commitment to national flexibility, a British priority, than to gold convertibility. The system had a glorious run from 1959 to 1971—a period of low, stable inflation and solid growth—but was ultimately held together by weak glue: capital controls and G-10 lending. All of the convertibility commitment credibility burden was borne by one country, the United States, which progressively lost the will to shoulder it beginning in the mid-1960s. When the French and the British threatened to cash in their excess dollars for gold in the summer of 1971, President Nixon shuttered the gold window for good.

Over a two-decade period beginning in 1979, European Union (EU) countries experienced periods of stability under a deutschmark peg, punctuated by episodes of forced devaluation when investor confidence in the political commitment to the system waned. The elimination of Bretton Woods–era capital controls made the commitment mechanism particularly vulnerable to speculative challenge, which knocked the least committed country, Britain, out of the system permanently in 1992. The adoption of a multinational European currency, the euro, by twelve EU countries in 1999 dramatically affirmed a powerful political commitment to a constitutionally mandated low-inflation regime—yet one that could still be undone at some future time if a hankering for monetary discretion should reemerge within its constituent nations.

Developing countries have also tried to substitute rule-based monetary policies for discretionary ones, first through the use of currency pegs and boards and then, more recently, in the wake of their collapses, through inflation targets. Will floating exchange rates and inflation targets be the answer, allowing them safely to integrate into the global market for goods and capital?

Sadly, the answer is no. Their money's no good there.

Ninety-seven percent of the outstanding securities placed in international markets are denominated in only five currencies: the dollar, the euro, the yen, the pound sterling, and the Swiss franc (the latter two of which are likely to disappear into euroland in our lifetime). Excluding the securities issued by the countries actually producing those currencies, the figure is still a remarkable 85 percent. The inability of most of the world to borrow abroad in its own currency has been termed the problem of "original sin."[20]

Why does the international market bless so few of the world's currencies, and damn the rest to domestic oblivion? The most obvious reason is the temptation governments have to reduce the value of their debt obligations through inflation. This represents not merely the risk of having a few percentage points shaved off the expected return, but a substantial loss of principal invested. Investors therefore demand securities denominated only in currencies for which there is a liquid international market and whose producers have a powerful self-interest in protecting a long-established reputation for sound money. Only a handful of currencies are considered as good as gold, or at least not a lot worse.

Countries that cannot successfully sell securities abroad in their own currencies have three choices. The first is to stay home, cutting themselves off from the global market for capital. The cost of this strategy is obvious: relying on a narrow base of domestic capital, which raises its price and therefore limits growth prospects, as does any form of capital rationing. The second is to market their securities abroad in dollars and other major currencies. The cost of this strategy has been made all too clear over the past two decades: the potential for currency collapse and financial crisis should foreign investors come to fear the country's inability to meet its foreign currency obligations. The government can mitigate this fear and protect against speculative attack by accumulating large amounts of international reserves, but this is a costly form of insurance. The third choice is to ditch the national currency entirely and to adopt the dollar or another major currency in its place.

The poster child for prudent financial market opening in the face of an unblessed currency is Chile. Chile did not cut itself off from world capital markets but instead tightly controlled the parameters under which foreign funds could come in and out. In combination with sound policies for regulating the behavior of domestic financial institutions, capital controls enabled Chile to weather the financial storms which buffeted much of Latin America in the 1990s. This does not mean, however, that Chile did not suffer for its original sin. Chile could have used foreign borrowing to help stabilize production and support consumption in the face of a steep decline in export earnings in 1998, but instead was obliged to cut imports by 22 percent, equivalent to nearly 6 percent of GDP, in order to balance its books. Barriers to capital importation also raised financing costs to Chilean firms.[21] The result was to move from boom to recession between 1997 and 1999, with GDP growth collapsing from 6.8 percent to −0.8 percent.[22] To be sure, this result may have been vastly better than what might have transpired had Chile left itself exposed to the vagaries of foreign investor confidence in its fiscal and monetary controls. It may, on the other hand, have been even better to have cleansed itself entirely of original sin and to have allowed dollarization to make its balance of payments with the world almost as meaningless as New York's balance of payments with California.

Exchange Rates

Exchange rates frequently deviate, often substantially, from those which could plausibly be justified by economic "fundamentals." The same can be concluded for the volatility in currency movements, which is often far in excess of the volatility in information about fundamentals. Furthermore, for the currencies of less developed countries in particular, large and rapid changes in value tend to be downward rather than upward.

These observations typically prompt charges of systematic "market failure" in international currency trading. It is tempting simply to conclude that traders of currencies are subject to a greater degree of whim, irrationality, or Keynesian "animal spirits" than traders of commodities less prone to precipitous price collapse, like gold or coffee. Yet it is important to recognize a fundamental difference between currencies and commodities. The existence of most of the world's currencies is wholly unrelated to any spontaneous demand for them; they are reflexively produced, and their use mandated, by national governments as a manifestation of sovereignty. The amount of so-called base money brought into supply is controlled not according to that predictable and durable motivation which drives producers of gold or coffee—profit—but according to motivations which change with the political inclinations of those temporarily holding charge of the money's management. The political element of currency production and supply management is so powerful and pervasive that we must be extremely wary of policy conclusions that ascribe the obvious, and frequently calamitous, failures of the world of national currencies to those who must decide, in their own interests, whether to hold or jettison them.

Some illustrations are in order. A government facing a low internal debt, for example, is more likely than one facing a high internal debt to pursue stable prices—that is, low inflation. A high internal debt gives government officials an incentive to reduce the cost of servicing the debt by increasing the supply of money—that is, to produce high inflation. Discerning the motivations of the government in managing a currency, however, is only a limited part of the challenge that individuals and institutions face in deciding whether to increase or reduce their holdings of the currency.

The mechanics of deliberately producing runaway inflation are simple, but the mechanics of producing low inflation are not. Some governments at some points in time believe that maintaining a certain exchange rate vis-à-vis the dollar or another major currency is the most important factor in sustaining low inflation. Some governments at some points in time believe that targeting values of other variables—such as the money supply, or nominal GDP growth, or inflation figures themselves—is the most important factor in sustaining low inflation. But since the internal and external values of the currency (that is, inflation and the exchange rate) ultimately rely on the *confidence* of individuals in the motivations and technical competence of those managing the currency, there is no mechanical formula for success in monetary policy. Currency may be more convenient than commodities, such as gold, to manage transactions among individuals. It may also provide benefits in terms of greater flexibility of response when major economic events—like an oil price rise, or a drought, or a gold-mining disaster—afflict the populace. But flexibility implies discretion, and discretion implies error, inconsistency, and malfeasance. So long as there is discretion in monetary policy, then, the vagaries of confidence will be the flimsy foundations on which a currency's internal and external values are sustained.

Halfhearted attempts to remove discretion can, however, themselves encourage wild ups and downs in currency values. Pegging the exchange rate to the dollar or other major currency offers traders the most valuable gift markets have to offer: free options. Governments that peg are telling the world they will buy their currency without limits should its external value fall below a certain preannounced level. As the exchange rate falls toward that level, speculators are magnetically drawn to the market, seeking to test the government's resolve in the face of limited foreign exchange reserves to support its commitment. Breaking this resolve, or depleting the government's reserves, can be enormously profitable. George Soros is reputed to have earned well over $1 billion speculating against the British pound as it fell toward its lower bound in the European Exchange Rate Mechanism in 1992. While speculators like Soros have been routinely demonized for their selling, they cannot do so profitably without willing government buyers on the other side. Wild currency movements are frequently the result of government hubris in creating fiat money and attempting to dictate to humanity what it shall be worth.

The Optimum Is the Enemy of the Good

Today's economic orthodoxy on how to choose a currency regime dates back to Robert Mundell's theory of optimum currency areas, or OCAs, published in 1961. The theory has been subjected to quite a few facelifts and Talmudic reinterpretations since its birth, but its practical message lives on: whether a nation should have its own currency with a flexible exchange rate or join a larger currency area depends on how integrated its goods and labor markets are with those of the proposed area.

Empirical analyses of the EU national economies prior to the creation of the eurozone generally concluded that integration of the constituent economies was insufficient, by the standards of OCA theory, to warrant the elimination of national currencies. Such studies have frequently been invoked as an economic defense of national currencies, much to the chagrin of Mundell himself, who has long supported a *world* currency.

Invoking OCA theory to justify the global constellation of national currencies should give rise to at least four obvious objections.

The first is that if nations make better currency areas than groups of nations, shouldn't we expect municipalities to make even better currency areas than nations? After all, labor and goods generally flow much more fluidly within towns than across them. Yet no economist seeking tenure will endorse subnational currencies.

The consistency between OCA defenses of national monies and the existence of a world already defined by national monies should naturally suggest that the degree of economic integration within and beyond national borders is itself largely a political result. And indeed, the OCA criteria turn out to be highly endogenous. That is, whether tests based on OCA theory conclude that a country is better off in or out of a currency area largely depends on whether the country is *already* in or out of it.

This gives rise to the second obvious challenge to the relevance of OCA theory: the evidence is overwhelming that the act of participating in a currency area *itself* increases trade and investment among the constituents. By dint of sharing a currency, Canadian provinces, for example, trade twenty times more among themselves than with U.S. states.[23] Combining the results of two dozen studies of currency unions suggests that they actually serve to *double* trade among the constituents, and that this trade effect dwarfs that of merely fixing exchange rates.[24] Furthermore, they do this primarily through trade creation with other union members, not diversion away from nonmembers.[25] Market integration, therefore, is more logically treated as a result of currency integration than as a touchstone for deciding whether to pursue it.

Third, OCA theory simply takes it as given that if a government opts to produce a freely floating national currency that it will be an "optimum" national currency. That is, it is assumed that the country will be able to enjoy the same benefits of current and capital account liberalization that, say, dollarization allows, because its monetary authority will be able to adapt monetary policy instantaneously and cope perfectly with any supply shocks. This is far removed from the reality of a world in which the internationally tradable currencies of all but the very richest countries have been routinely plagued with bouts of ruinous inflation and depreciation. This is the reason so many Latin American countries are de facto dollarized, meaning that their citizens have opted to hold dollars as a store of value rather than the national money introduced by their governments.

Finally, OCA theory stands out from the entire body of microeconomic theory in presuming that consumer preferences are irrelevant. Thus even if every one of a country's citizens chooses to save in dollars and demand them in payment, OCA theory is no less likely to be invoked to conclude that dollarization is against the country's economic interests. This obviously divorces the concept of a country from its citizens entirely and elevates it to a transparently absurd level of abstraction.

In the late 1980s, a common joke in Poland ran, "What do America and Poland have in common? In America, you can buy everything in dollars and nothing in zlotys. In Poland, it is exactly the same." If there were a macroeconomist's retort, it would probably be: "Stupid Poles. Do they really think America and Poland are an optimum currency area?"

OCA theory provides the flimsiest of intellectual foundations for maintaining national currencies. Economic integration as a prerequisite for currency integration makes little sense when currency integration is itself such a powerful enabling force behind economic integration. No single monetary policy will ever be optimal for all regions at any given point in time, but optimality is not achievable in any case. If we were to refashion the globe into economic regions across which flexible exchange rates could perform a textbook stabilizing role,[26] these regions would, unfortunately, be far from "optimum political areas." And it is politics which ultimately determines borders, not OCA theory.

Even in such a refashioned world, flexible exchange rates would only be stabilizing under the Keynesian assumption that currency depreciation painlessly absorbs supply shocks that would otherwise result in wage inflation or unemployment.[27] The exchange rate operates, in this view, as a "fooling device"[28] through which the authorities engineer lower real wages at 30,000 feet, well above the heads of oblivious workers. Yet the postwar evidence shows that the device does not work. When depreciation brings inflation, workers are neither ignorant of the effect nor stoic in confronting it. They insist on wage indexation, thereby fueling inflation and unemployment. Furthermore, there is a double whammy in the capital market, where the surprise devaluation option translates into an interest rate premium and, therefore, a higher cost of capital. There is no Keynesian free lunch in flexible exchange rates.

Dirty Floating

A policy of allowing the exchange rate to float freely sounds simple, as it is, in essence, a commitment to do precisely nothing deliberately to affect the external value of the currency. The idea is that if the monetary authority focuses myopically on controlling inflation, then economic stability will take care of itself, whatever happens in the currency markets.

In reality, benign neglect of the currency markets is well nigh impossible where any significant de facto dollarization has already taken hold. Inflation targeting itself requires greater attention to the nominal exchange rate the greater the degree of "pass through" from the exchange rate to domestic inflation. This pass through will be greater the greater the prevalence of dollar pricing in the economy.

But inflation control is only one critical objective that requires attention to the exchange rate and the policy measures that affect it. Protecting the financial sector is another. Companies, particularly those doing business abroad, will typically wish to borrow from their banks in dollars, which have an added attraction of a lower nominal interest rate. The greater the percentage of those companies' earnings in local currency, the greater the risk they will default on their dollar loans if the local currency depreciates. What is currency risk to the companies is credit risk to the banks, and what is credit risk to the banks is deposit risk to the savers who ultimately finance the loans. Currency risk, therefore, can undermine the foundations of the entire economy.

Faced with this fact, the monetary authorities have a strong incentive to try to stabilize the exchange rate. And knowing that the monetary authority has this incentive, companies will be further encouraged to borrow in dollars, thus inducing even greater financial dollarization and even greater incentive for the authorities to prevent depreciation.

But companies are not the only domestic actors likely to borrow heavily in dollars. The government itself is likely to have a substantial amount of dollar-denominated sovereign debt outstanding, given the inability of the vast majority of the world's governments to find willing foreign holders of domestic currency bonds. Potential foreign lenders fear that the governments will, in effect, partially default on domestic currency debt by devaluing, thus encouraging those lenders to demand dollar-denominated debt. Once the government has built up a substantial stock of dollar debt, it has yet greater incentive to manage the exchange rate.

The result is that almost no freely floating currencies exist outside of textbooks, as the growing internationalization of the dollar (and the euro and the yen) has compelled governments, for reasons both economic and political, to float dirty. Witness the relentless buildup of reserves and uncannily stable currencies in the Asian emerging markets since the crisis of 1997–98. From the beginning of 2002 to September 2003, Asian reserves grew by a staggering $546 billion. Combined with abnormally high volatility in interest rates (nominal and real), reserves, and monetary aggregates, these data indicate a systematic procyclical monetary policy guided by exchange rate targeting.[29] In the words of Calvo and Reinhart, "If they are floating, they are doing so with a life jacket."[30] Not surprisingly, developing countries don't actually see economic benefits from operating an "independent" monetary policy beyond the absence of massive speculative attacks on their currency that come with an explicit exchange rate peg.

The textbook case for floating a national currency is founded on the stabilizing effects of using the exchange rate to keep domestic interest rates from being whipsawed by movements in foreign rates, and the ability to lower rates to counteract recessions (and raise them to moderate booms). Yet the evidence is precisely the opposite: that under floating regimes, domestic interest rates are *more* sensitive to foreign rates, and, perversely, are more likely to go up than down during a recession.[31] Indeed, in developing countries a procyclical interest rate policy has clearly replaced foreign exchange intervention as the preferred means of taming currency movements.[32] These findings on their own cannot, of course, tell us whether developing country monetary authorities are incompetent or merely ineffective, but they do suggest clearly that they are unable to do what we know they must do if they are to derive any benefit out of monetary independence.

Calvo and Reinhart (2000) have termed the unwillingness of govern-ments to leave determination of exchange rates to the market "fear of floating." Fear it may be, but in a world in which large and sudden exchange rate movements frequently wreak havoc with economic stability, even exchange rate paranoids must reckon with enemies.

Only a Dollar Is a Dollar

Tropical experiments have had their time on the stage; they should now give way to hard money as the single best development strategy.
—Rudi Dornbusch[33]

The Asian crisis shattered what had become a near orthodoxy in developing country monetary policy: that low inflation and capital-market integration could be installed overnight through pegged exchange rate regimes. Argentina showed that even currency boards were dangerously vulnerable unless dollar reserves were sufficient to cover not only the monetary base but the private sector's net dollar liabilities. Essentially, exchange rate prom-ises are worthless. A peso is not a dollar, and never was. Even in the boom times, Argentine banks had to pay a premium of about two percentage points in order to attract peso rather than dollar deposits (see figure 2).

Crisis in the peg church has led to a schism among the following. Most have abandoned faith in the dollar and have called for an existential float. These disillusioned souls have decided that the spark of the divine resides within each country, in the form of the domestic inflation rate. Target it faithfully and exclusively, and all will be well.

Dollarizers, on the other side, have condemned the floaters as idol-aters, worshiping at the altar of false graven monies. Only a dollar is a dollar, and the people need dollars. Local currencies keep the people iso-lated from the global capital market and give them a false sense of eco-nomic security. Inflation targeting without guidance from the dollar is a chimera, monetary independence a dangerous myth.

The Benefits of Dollarization

The globalization phenomenon of the late twentieth century was built on the voluntary and uncoordinated acceptance of the dollar as a

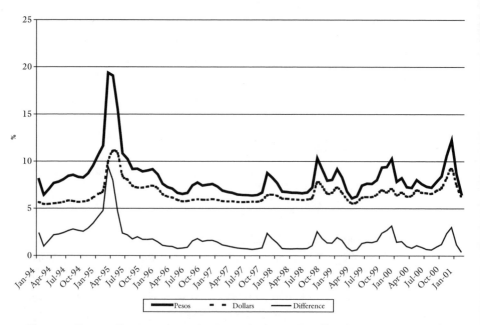

Figure 2. Interest Rates on Argentine Deposits (30–59 Day Term). Source: Antinolfi and Keister 2001; Central Bank of Argentina

global medium of exchange, just as its predecessor of the late nineteenth century was built on the pound sterling and gold. Globalization's Achilles' heel has been the fatal association of national monetary autonomy with national sovereignty, which has led to a proliferation of unwanted currencies in the international marketplace, each of which is tied to the dollar by nothing more than serially discredited promises of instantaneous convertibility at fixed or semifixed values.

This state of affairs is not the result of policy decisions. It is, rather, a reflection of the fact that monetary sovereignty in international transactions lies with individuals and private entities which determine for themselves what money shall be considered an acceptable store of value. As a spontaneous order, rather than an imposed regime, this dollar-based system of global exchange is neither fair nor unfair, just nor unjust. Fairness and justice are attributes of human conduct, and not of states of affairs which no identifiable action or decision has brought about or even intended.[34]

The continued assertion of national monetary sovereignty by the vast majority of the world's governments should no longer be considered an economic choice, but a wholly political one. And a largely self-destructive one at that. The case for national money based on considerations of economic welfare is simply too flimsy to sustain in the face of so much evidence against it. That perceptions of what functions are properly within the sovereign sphere of individuals, states, and international entities can change radically over mere decades is clearly evidenced by the evolution of the EU since its founding in 1957. The creation of the euro is merely its most tangible manifestation. We believe that the time is ripe, economically and politically, for the global denationalization of money.

The economic benefits of international currency consolidation would be considerable. Fewer monies would lead to greatly increased trade, financial integration, productivity, and real incomes. And by any reasonable standard, global dollarization would mean an immediate and substantial improvement in the performance of perhaps two-thirds of the world's national monetary regimes. The "central bank movement," a product of the collapse of the gold standard in the 1920s, has been a demonstrative failure for developing nations. At the time of the movement's birth, to quote Mundell, "no one anticipated that [central banks] would be transmogrified into instruments of inflation, handmaidens of the fiscal authorities."[35] Yet they have been.

Dollarized countries have been shown to produce vastly superior inflation records vis-à-vis comparable control-group nondollarizers.[36] Economists who have long preached the importance of developing domestic financial markets in order to reduce dependence on dollar financing[37] would get their desired effect by abandoning their cause. Dollar financing is clearly the right recipe for a dollar economy, and the ingredients are the most abundant, coveted, and mobile in the global capital market. Risk management in dollarized economies becomes vastly simpler and cheaper, as such economies are fully integrated into the global dollar-based derivatives markets. And regardless of what their governments do, citizens in developing countries will, rationally, continue to hold more and more of their savings, particularly long-term assets such as insurance annuities, in dollars as such investment opportunities become available to them.[38]

The Costs of Dollarization

LOSS OF MONETARY POLICY The loss of an independent monetary policy is the most widely invoked objection to dollarization. But since the Holy Grail of monetary policy is to get interest rates down to the lowest level consistent with low and stable inflation, this argument is, for most of the world, frivolous. How many Latin American central banks can cut interest rates below those in New York?[39] The average *real* (inflation-adjusted) lending rate in Latin America is about 20 percent. In Brazil, it averaged 60 percent between 1999 and 2003. Naturally, rates this high cripple business investment and worsen fiscal deficits. Meanwhile, the dollarized country in Latin America with the *highest* real lending rate is Ecuador, at a minuscule 4.4 percent in 2003.

One must therefore ask what possible net gain to the national economy developing country central banks can hope to achieve from the ability to guide nominal local rates up and down on a discretionary basis. It is like choosing a Hyundai with manual transmission over a Lexus with automatic. The former gives the driver more control, but at the cost of inferior performance under any condition.

Consider how "independent monetary policy" operated in Latin America in 1998, as the region came under stress owing to commodity price shocks triggered by the Asian and Russian financial crises. Countries with flexible exchange rate regimes—Chile, Colombia, Mexico, and Peru—not only failed to use such flexibility as a shock absorber, but actually *raised interest rates dramatically* to defend their currencies against attack. In fact, real interest rates in Latin America over the past quarter century have been *more highly correlated* with U.S. rates for flexible rate regimes than for fixed.[40] Thus independent monetary policy is not a shock absorber, but a shock enhancer. Furthermore, real interest rates in Latin America are strongly correlated with real depreciation rates, reflecting the heightened risk associated with the region's currencies from using devaluation as a tool of monetary expansion.[41] These punishingly high real interest rates severely damage the region's economic growth.

It is important to note that inflation itself, the bugbear of developing economies, contributes directly to the generation of currency mismatches, and therefore financial crises. Countries with higher or more volatile inflation issue more foreign debt and have less developed local bond markets.[42] Inflation is the single most critical variable explaining the degree to which dollars are used in domestic transactions,[43] making it the first deadly step on the path to currency crisis.

As regions such as the Americas become more economically integrated, in terms of sharing in the production of final goods, the classical case for independent monetary policies and flexible exchange rates disintegrates. Any shocks to aggregate demand for final goods affect all those who contribute to their supply in the same fashion, thereby negating whatever Keynesian shock absorption effect an exchange rate might provide, even in theory.[44]

LOSS OF LENDER OF LAST RESORT Opponents of dollarization often argue that it substitutes banking crises for currency crises. It is true that the elimination of the national currency precludes the central bank from printing money to bail out domestic banks. Yet designing a monetary regime on this basis is like building a house with removable supporting beams, under the logic that they might conveniently be used to prop up a sofa when fat guests visit.

The track record on bank bailouts in Latin America, southeast Asia, and, most recently, Turkey, is awful. They put confidence in the foundation of economic activity, the currency, at direct risk. The very possibility of bank bailouts not backed by foreign reserves represents a dangerous public underwriting of bank lending behavior, thereby making the systemic crisis which a lender of last resort is supposed to manage far more likely to materialize. Studies do, in fact, suggest strongly that the presence of a domestic lender of last resort is itself a *cause* of excess volatility in emerging financial markets as well as currency crises. [45] Bank bailout mechanisms should be financed transparently through risk-adjusted deposit insurance premia paid for by the banks themselves, and not after the fact by surreptitiously creating new public debt on the books of the central bank.

It is furthermore critical to note that the entire intellectual apparatus of a lender of last resort premised on printing money is a nonsense in an open economy. A central bank printing money in excess of demand for it will trigger an outflow of funds, generally through the capital account, which leads directly to depletion of the central bank's dollar reserves. This has been well documented in the case of Brazil between 1998 and 2003, where the central bank's dollar reserves fell in line with monetary expansion and rose with contraction.[46] As the Brazilian central bank cannot actually print reais without losing dollar reserves, its lender of last resort powers are illusory. This was further illustrated during the Ukrainian election chaos in December 2004: central bank dollar reserves plummeted as depositors pulled their money out of banks and immediately converted them to dollars.[47]

A central bank faced with a financial crisis needs *dollars*. Thus, as Guillermo Calvo astutely noted, central banks are no longer lenders of last resort. They are *borrowers* of last resort.

LOSS OF SEIGNIORAGE   When a country has its own currency, its government earns interest on the foreign reserves it receives from those who buy the local currency, yet pays no interest to holders of the currency. The profit it earns from issuing non-interest-bearing local currency in return for interest-bearing foreign assets (like U.S. Treasury bills) is known as seigniorage.

How big is this profit? It depends on the accounting measure chosen. If you multiply the dollar value of the currency in circulation by the interest rate on U.S. T-bills, you will get a figure equivalent to roughly 0.2 percent of GDP for an average Latin American country. Alternatively, you could multiply the dollar value of the monetary base, which is greater than the value of currency in circulation, by the domestic inflation or interest rate (which is usually much higher than the T-bill rate). This will naturally give you a larger figure, estimated at 0.5 percent for precrisis Argentina to a substantial 7.4% for Ecuador.[48] This second measure of seigniorage profit is frequently cited by opponents of dollarization, who argue that giving up the national currency is too costly.

Too costly to whom? is the question that should be asked. Calculating the so-called flow cost of lost seigniorage using the local currency inflation (or interest) rate presumes that it is a good thing for a country that its government can profit from inflation. Yet inflation is a tax paid by the citizens, so there is no free lunch to the nation as a whole. Much of the seigniorage profit is, therefore, at best illusory and at worst a sign of damagingly high inflation. Governments that rely heavily on the inflation tax are more likely to impose capital controls on their citizens, presumably as a means of preventing them from escaping the tax by saving abroad.[49]

If a country dollarizes, there is also a one-time cost from the need to obtain sufficient dollars to replace the local currency in circulation. This so-called stock cost is estimated at 4–5 percent of GDP for the average Latin American economy.[50] The more de facto dollarized a country is, based on its citizens having already substituted dollars for local money, the lower this stock cost is. Furthermore, there are powerful offsetting direct monetary benefits to dollarization—in particular, lower foreign reserve requirements and lower public debt service costs—which can, on their own, more than offset costs in lost seigniorage.

Nonetheless, loss of seigniorage represents the strongest argument against dollarization. Fortunately, the United States has it in its power to make the argument irrelevant, at no cost to American taxpayers. As lost seigniorage to a dollarizing government is revenue to the U.S. Treasury, this revenue can and should simply be rebated. Precisely such a proposal was the centerpiece of the 2000 U.S. International Monetary Stability Act, which unfortunately never made its way into law (see chap. 7).

LOSS OF A SOVEREIGN SYMBOL If a country's citizens have already exhibited a revealed preference for dollars in their savings and transaction behavior, they are clearly indicating that they consider money to be a private rather than a government matter. Surely it is better, then, to look elsewhere for patriotic outlets.

Is dollarization in any sense undemocratic, a violation of popular sovereignty? Certainly not. In fact, most policymaking in democracies involves institutions designed specifically to insulate it from popular pressure.[51] Dollarization is akin to constitutional laws barring certain actions by government officials, such as property seizure.

In more mundane terms, imagine a referendum posing the following simple question: Would you rather be paid in dollars or pesos? (assuming a national currency called the peso). If the majority would answer "dollars," there is no case grounded in democratic principle for maintaining the peso. For to say, "I wish to be paid in dollars, but to keep the peso" is to say, "I wish debts to me to be paid in dollars, but my debts to others to be paid in pesos." Such a shaft-thy-neighbor principle cannot be translated into sound public policy.

Alternatives to Dollarization

CAPITAL CONTROLS Blocking access to foreign capital raises local capital costs in precisely the same way that steel quotas or tariffs raise manufacturing costs for local steel users. Cheering on the development of local-currency capital markets is fine as far it goes, but local markets are no more an alternative to international markets than gardens are an alternative to supermarkets. Furthermore, governments don't make private capital markets any more than eBay makes auctions. Building the field is easy. Making them come is not. It takes a reputation for low and stable inflation, not capital controls and patriotic sentiments, to inspire local-currency bond trading.[52] Finally, if capital controls prevent financial crises, the root reason is that they prevent mass selling of the local currency. The local-currency financial flows that occur *within* a country—from richer to poorer regions, from stagnant to growing regions—are rarely themselves attacked as destabilizing. The clear implication is that legal dollarization simply localizes all financial flows with other parts of the world that use the dollar, making them no more inherently destabilizing than flows between New York and West Virginia.

FREE FLOAT A nice idea, as are lots of ideas expressed algebraically. But free floats don't exist in reality, and for good reason. In developing countries, targeting inflation, or indeed any measure of economic stability, positively requires attention to the exchange rate. This is especially the case where de facto dollarization has already set in, in order to guard against mass private-sector default and bankruptcy, as it has been shown historically to be virtually impossible to de-dollarize an economy without massive capital flight and a collapse in bank credit to the private sector.[53]

PEG The harder the peg, the more attractive it is to a Soros. Speculators live for free options, and central banks that peg offer the biggest. Furthermore, countries that peg have a higher incidence of unhedged private-sector dollar borrowing, thereby encouraging crisis and worsening its effects when it comes.[54]

CURRENCY BOARD Will the central bank accumulate sufficient dollar reserves to back the private sector's dollar liabilities as well as the government's? If it does, the opportunity cost of the idle reserve capital may swamp the seigniorage loss from outright dollarization. If it doesn't, the board has all the drawbacks of a hard peg, as Argentina learned so painfully. Currency boards provide the maximum possible incentive for unhedged private-sector dollar borrowing, thereby ensuring financial disaster if and when they collapse.

The Experience of Dollarizers

A list of countries and territories which are officially dollarized is provided in table 1. Those using other (foreign) currencies are listed in table 2.

Although dollarizers have been mostly small countries, the record on economic stability is impressive, whether the measure be inflation, interest rates, real exchange rates, capital flows, or bank failures. Ecuador, which dollarized in 2000, following a period of devastating capital flight, saw bank deposits and financial stability restored rapidly. Ecuador's inflation rate in 2004, just over 3 percent, is among the lowest in Latin America. El Salvador, which dollarized in 2001 under far more auspicious conditions, now has a minuscule real lending rate of about 3 percent, compared with 20 percent on average in Latin America.

Dollarizers further have more developed financial systems, featuring staples of middle-class American life, such as 15–30 year fixed-rate mortgages, which are unavailable elsewhere in the developing world. Foreign exchange transaction costs, hedging costs, and bank reserve costs are all considerably lower (about 5 percent of GDP lower in Panama).[55] Private property is more secure, owing to the elimination of inflation and devaluation taxes and the very rationale for exchange controls and forced conversions (as Mexico imposed on dollar bank deposits in 1982, and Argentina in 2001). Fiscal transparency is greater owing to lesser incentives to disguise a lack of dollar reserves through derivative transactions (as Thailand did in 1997). In short, although dollarization is not an economic miracle drug, it is demonstrably the most secure foundation upon which a developing country can integrate its economy and financial system with that of the wider world.

Table 1.   Countries and territories using the U.S. dollar

Economy	Population	GDP ($bn)	Political status	Currency	Since
American Samoa	57,902	0.50	U.S. territory	U.S. dollar	1899
British Virgin Islands	22,187	0.32	British dependency	U.S. dollar	1973
East Timor	1,019,252	0.44	Independent	U.S. dollar	2000
Ecuador	13,212,742	45.48	Independent	U.S. dollar	2000
El Salvador	6,587,541	30.99	Independent	U.S. dollar	2001
Guam	166,090	3.20	U.S. territory	U.S. dollar	1898
Marshall Islands	57,738	0.12	Independent	U.S. dollar	1944
Micronesia	108,155	0.28	Independent	U.S. dollar	1944
Northern Mariana Islands	78,252	0.90	U.S. commonwealth	U.S. dollar	1944
Palau	20,016	0.17	Independent	U.S. dollar	1944
Panama	3,000,463	18.62	Independent	U.S. dollar, own balboa coins	1904
Pitcairn Island	46	NA	British dependency	New Zealand, U.S. dollars	1800s
Puerto Rico	3,897,960	65.28	U.S. commonwealth	U.S. dollar	1899
Turks and Caicos Islands	19,956	0.23	British colony	U.S. dollar	1973
U.S. Virgin Islands	108,775	2.50	U.S. territory	U.S. dollar	1934

Source: http://users.erols.com/kurrency/dllrlist.htm; CIA World Factbook.

Table 2.   Countries and territories using foreign currencies other than the U.S. dollar

Economy	Population	GDP ($bn)	Political status	Currency	Since
Andorra	69,865	1.30	Independent	euro (formerly French franc, Spanish peseta), own coins	1278
Cocos (Keeling) Islands	629	NA	Australian external territory	Australian dollar	1995
Cook Islands	21,200	0.11	New Zealand self-governing territory	New Zealand dollar	1995
Cyprus, Northern	200,000	1.22	de facto independent	Turkish lira	1974
Greenland	56,384	1.10	Danish self-governing region	Danish krone	before 1800
Kiribati	100,798	0.08	Independent	Australian dollar, own coins	1943
Kosovo	1,700,000	1.46	U.N. administration	euro	1999
Liechtenstein	33,436	0.83	Independent	Swiss franc	1921
Monaco	32,270	0.87	Independent	euro (formerly French franc)	1865
Montenegro	616,258	2.00	Semi-independent	euro (partly "DM-ized" since 1999)	2002
Nauru	12,809	0.06	Independent	Australian dollar	1914
Niue	2,156	0.01	New Zealand self-governing territory	New Zealand dollar	1901
Norfolk Island	1,841	NA	Australian external territory	Australian dollar	before 1900?
San Marino	28,503	0.94	Independent	euro (formerly Italian lira), own coins	1897
Tokelau	1,405	0.00	New Zealand territory	New Zealand dollar	1926

Table 2.   (*cont'd*)

Economy	Population	GDP ($bn)	Political status	Currency	Since
Tuvalu	11,468	0.01	Independent	Australian dollar, own coins	1892
Vatican City	921	NA	Independent	euro (formerly Italian lira), own coins	1929

Source: http://users.erols.com/kurrency/dllrlist.htm; http://www.trncgov.com/abouttrnc_demographics.htm; http://www.gesource.ac.uk/worldguide/html/1073.html; CIA World Factbook.

The IMF and Dollarization

The IMF was created after World War II specifically to support a dollar-centered world, not a world of over a hundred autarkic currencies. The simple idea was that the Fund could assist countries in maintaining a fixed rate to the dollar with limited short-term financing to ease temporary balance of payments problems.

Over the past two decades, this world has changed beyond recognition and has placed demands on the Fund it cannot possibly meet. The Bretton Woods system of fixed exchange rates enabled countries to control their interest rates while keeping their currency rate locked to the dollar (and gold) only because capital flows were restricted. Yet as governments and private institutions in developing countries began seeking international capital in the 1980s, many of their central banks and treasuries sought simultaneously to maintain both low domestic interest rates and a stable dollar exchange rate, with disastrous results for their economies.

This put the IMF in an impossible position, from which it has been struggling unsuccessfully to adapt or to extricate itself ever since. In affirming the benefits of international capital, the Fund did no more than ratify the common sense that its growing clientele had already signed on to unilaterally: that access to a larger pool of capital lowered its cost. Problems emerged, however, when these governments also adopted dollar pegs to keep their exchange rates stable and simultaneously to anchor low inflation expectations domestically. Despite muted concerns that Fund staff expressed periodically over the dangers of overvaluation, it was impossible politically to challenge these policies openly, as to do so risked undermining their apparent success by scaring off the eager foreign investors.

By the time investors, domestic as well as foreign, did eventually smell whiffs of default risk in the exchange rate, it was too late for the Fund to do anything other than try to contain the flames. As a bank, the only way it could do so was through a combination of loans to forestall default on existing debts and policy conditionality to ensure that the governments would emerge capable of repaying the new debt to the Fund.

While the Fund has admitted mistakes in extending traditional conditionality, based on transparent requirements for client fiscal probity, into peripheral and highly sensitive areas such as corporate governance and "cronyism," it remains an ineluctable principle of banking that the bank must control its clients' behavior sufficiently to ensure that loans can be repaid and recycled into future loans. Even a bank without a profit-making mission must do so successfully in order to perpetuate itself. That the Fund has come popularly to be seen, and indeed seeks to be seen, as an institution with a humanitarian mission, however, assured that it would subsequently become popularly reviled in appearing to impose suffering on the poor in their moments of crisis. This was the case even where it should have been clear that the crisis governments would have had to impose far harsher economic measures to avert default were IMF loans unavailable to give them breathing space for longer-term reforms to take hold.

Yet the Fund has been subjected to another indictment, equally inevitable, from the right of the political spectrum. In lending massive sums of money to indebted governments, the Fund is wide open to the charge that it is "bailing out" irresponsible private lenders with public funds and thereby encouraging even more such irresponsible borrowing and lending in the future. This is known as the problem of moral hazard, which refers to the phenomenon whereby people who are insured against the consequences of risky activity will engage in more of it.

In the relative calm of the aftermath of debt crises in Argentina and Brazil, the Fund began concentrating its energies on limiting future demand for its politically charged lending facilities by trying to transform itself into a sort of international bankruptcy court. This initiative, known as the Sovereign Debt Reduction Mechanism (SDRM), seeks not to prevent governments from defaulting, but to limit the economic damage of default by giving creditors more incentive to reach a speedy compromise on debt restructuring and injecting a mechanism to impose one where such compromise is not forthcoming. The attraction to the Fund itself is obvious, as success in such an initiative would keep its lending practices out of the crosshairs of the antiglobalization left and the anti-moral-hazard right when the next crisis hits. Unfortunately for the Fund, the proposal has been subjected to powerful criticism from both private lenders and sovereign borrowers, the former believing it will lead to more defaults and worse terms for creditors, and the latter that it will lead to higher borrowing costs.

Whether this scheme or some similar one is eventually implemented, more or less widely, the Fund's existential crisis will not end. The attractions of international capital will only increase as the financial services industry continues to expand, increase efficiency, and reduce global capital costs. Developed country supply of investable dollars and developing country demand for them will inevitably increase, to the clear net benefit of both. But it is also inevitable that in such a world, ever more financially integrated, but in which 98 percent of the currencies are unmarketable across borders, ever more severe currency mismatches will afflict ever more national balance sheets. Many more governments will throw off the shackles of capital controls, and most of those will prosper for most of the time. But financial crises will continue to emerge so long as governments continue to inject autarkic national currencies into internationally integrated national economies. In such an environment, there is every prospect that demands on IMF lending facilities will not only overstrain its lending capacity, but fatally undermine its political legitimacy on both the left and right.

Given such a bleak vision of the IMF's future, we see a saving grace in this jarringly modest comment from Stanley Fischer in May 2000, when he was still the Fund's first deputy managing director: "When you get right down to it, the benefits of having your own currency are much smaller than we used to think, especially for countries that already to a considerable extent are using the dollar."[56] We would add only that the costs are also much greater.

7

GLOBAL CAPITAL FLOWS AND
U.S. FOREIGN POLICY

Just after the Clinton administration approved a $20 billion line of credit to Mexico in 1995, then-Treasury Undersecretary Lawrence Summers is said to have quipped that his human capital was now denominated in pesos.[1] Humor often captures the gravity of a situation in a way that gravity itself cannot.

Far more than $20 billion rested on the fate of the peso. Barely a year before, the North American Free Trade Agreement had come into effect, heralding what was supposed to be a new era of economic and political progress in a country that had known little of either. Now, further collapse in the beleaguered peso threatened to trigger hyperinflation in Mexico, destroying companies, livelihoods, and savings and plunging millions into abject poverty. A fragile emerging democracy was itself in the balance. Looking out more widely, then-Treasury Secretary Robert Rubin observed that "with implementation of the North American Free Trade Agreement (NAFTA), Mexico was hailed as a role model for developing countries pursuing economic reform. The public failure of that model could deal an enormous setback to the spread of market-based economic reforms and globalization."[2]

The immediate economic effect of collapse north of the Rio Grande would have been a potent but manageable jolt to a rising U.S. economy. Beyond the short term and beyond American borders, however, the landscape appeared much bleaker. Economic devastation in Mexico would trigger waves of northbound migrants far beyond what was already seen as a significant social and political problem in the United States. The prospect of further devaluations southward in Latin America would spook already jittery investors, bringing that giant sucking sound of capital flowing back north. The New World Order, which was to be founded on free peoples and free trade, would crumble under the weight of fear, economic pessimism, and insecurity. All this must have weighed on the mind of a Treasury undersecretary who, in the minds of his congressional critics, was committing American treasure to bail out greedy banks and corrupt foreigners.

By the standards of contemporary currency crises, this one had a happy ending. Mexico did not collapse or default, global economic integration hobbled forward, and the Treasury undersecretary emerged with his human capital intact. But the episode only presaged more currency crises to come in places like Thailand, Korea, Malaysia, Indonesia, Russia, Turkey, Argentina, and Brazil, each of which serving to fuel a powerful global popular backlash against trade, capital movements, and economic liberalism generally.

So much is at stake for the United States in finding a way to prevent the next wave of currency crises while resurrecting popular support for a world based on economic interdependence and openness. If the governments of nations perched precariously between authoritarianism and liberal democracy come to see their own legitimacy enhanced through the wealth-generating effects of foreign trade and investment, they will likewise develop a stake in conflict avoidance and stability in international affairs. If, on the other hand, they come to see domestic social chaos as the inevitable result of liberalization, they will seek to ground their legitimacy in confrontation with an emergent American-led international order. As critical as American military power may be to protecting a way of life that has made American citizenship so coveted globally, the soft power projected through the internationalization of norms supporting peaceful conflict resolution among governments and free economic exchange among people is eminently more effective and reliable over the long term. And there is no greater threat to this soft power than a sense among the vast populace of the world's poorer nations that such norms serve to enrich America *at their expense*. Preventing the recurrent collapse of currencies upon which national economies are, however unfortunately, currently built is central to the task of legitimizing a liberal international economic order among this skeptical populace.

Foreign Policy versus Economics?

The debates within the Clinton administration over how best to deal with currency crises in Mexico, South Korea, Indonesia, Russia, and elsewhere might give an outside observer the impression that decisions had to be taken on the grounds of *either* foreign policy concerns *or* economic concerns. *Either* the United States backed South Korea with financial assistance and thereby kept the North from exploiting its neighbor's instability,[3] *or* the United States withheld such assistance in the cause of saving American treasure and discouraging excessive, destabilizing lending and investment abroad in the future.

Whereas both concerns may be valid, each of these lenses for viewing the problem is defective. The foreign policy lens is fuzzy unless adjusted for economics, as financial assistance without the right conditionality means lower odds of achieving the foreign policy ends. The economics lens, on the other hand, is useless unless focused on foreign policy priorities, as the likelihood of different financial outcomes is only a meaningful guide to action to the extent that the relative strategic importance of different ends guides the decision process.

What does this mean in practice?

The State Department may wish the commitment of financial assistance to an ally to serve as a signal to hostile nations that America will not afford them the opportunity to exploit economic instability. This is a wholly valid purpose to which American funds should be devoted. Yet to know this purpose is not a sufficient basis upon which to commit funds. State must know, for example, how such funds should be disbursed to and committed within the recipient country to ensure the best possible chance of success in stabilizing it. If the country's monetary policy needs to be changed and government expenditures reallocated or reduced in order to maximize the chances for successful financial stabilization, then American foreign policy ends will not be served by allowing the money to be directed instead to recapitalizing politically connected banks and other enterprises. It may be objected that those with economic expertise often get these judgments wrong, but this is hardly a reason to rely on economic ignorance.

If no feasible amount of financial assistance, on the other hand, holds out a realistic hope of preventing a country from defaulting on its external debt, then American foreign policy ends are unlikely to be served by committing funds purely as a symbolic gesture. After all, precipitating future crises by signaling to investors and other governments that America will underwrite capital flows to strategically significant countries represents a foreign policy risk itself. Moral hazard should not be a matter of concern just to bankers.

Consider now the economics lens. Would it be meaningful for Treasury to criticize a proposed $20 billion loan guarantee on the grounds that it had only a 50 percent chance of being repaid—without regard to whether the country is Fiji or Iraq? Is the risk of injecting moral hazard into international lending a compelling reason to reject a $20 billion loan guarantee— without regard to whether a friendly government is likely to be replaced by a hostile one in the absence of such a guarantee? The answer to both questions is obviously no, as in both cases there are foreign policy considerations which dictate whether a given financial risk is worth taking.

Although it might be a slight caricature of crisis decision making within the Clinton administration to say that it pitted blind bailout doves in State against deaf moral hazard hawks in Treasury, the tensions between the two groups were palpable. In the words of Deputy National Security Adviser James Steinberg,

> The extreme version of the argument national security types like me were making was that [a major bailout] was worth trying even if it was certain to fail. That isn't what we were saying; it's just the extreme interpretation. The extreme version of the Treasury argument was, don't do it unless it's certain to succeed. What was mutually arrived at was that it was no good to do something if it was absolutely futile. We accepted that there had to be some probability of success, and Treasury accepted that it didn't have to be just a high probability. If there was some

chance it would succeed—even if it was less than fifty-fifty, there was political value in having tried.[4]

Tensions were particularly high during the Korean financial crisis. Steinberg, allied with Secretary of State Madeleine Albright, was firm on the need for significant U.S. and IMF financial support. "This president is not going to look like Jimmy Carter," he insisted, referring to the former president's proposed troop reductions in Korea in the 1970s, which sparked vocal criticism throughout Asia.[5] Treasury Secretary Rubin, however, was much more circumspect, fearing that the IMF's credibility would be squandered if intervention failed and the financial markets lost confidence in its crisis management. He described decision making during the Korean financial crisis this way:

> For understandable reasons, we at Treasury and the foreign policy people in the administration looked at the issue from somewhat different perspectives. Madeleine and the other foreign policy advisers . . . were mainly worried about our relationship with a crucially important military ally, as well as national security issues. They thought any instability in South Korea might encourage a reaction from the North, where troops had gone to some heightened state of alert. Their view was that we economic types were insufficiently focused on geopolitical concerns and that the United States needed to move quickly to show support for South Korea through the IMF and a backup loan from the [Exchange Stabilization Fund]. . . . I felt strongly that if economic stability wasn't reestablished, our geopolitical goals wouldn't be accomplished either. . . . Committing the IMF and ourselves to a show of financial support for South Korea without an adequate commitment to reform might even make it less likely that South Korea would get back on track, because providing money without strong conditions would reduce our leverage in getting the country to adopt a program that would work.[6]

Rubin describes even greater tensions during the Russian financial crisis:

> One problem in this episode was that the people in the geopolitical sphere tended not to relate fully to the issues in the economic

> sphere, and vice versa. Even after the Duma vote [against reforms that were conditions for continued IMF lending], members of the Clinton foreign policy team were still very focused on trying to find a way to help Russia. . . . there was a lot of pressure on [Treasury] to proceed with less conditionality. I recognized the validity of the argument about the need to appear helpful even if additional support was exceedingly unlikely to do any good. But I believed very strongly that the risks on the other side were greater—so strongly that I felt that if they wanted to get another Treasury Secretary who would use the ESF, or who would try to force the IMF to act, that was fine with me.[7]

While concerned that Treasury was often insufficiently attuned to foreign policy priorities, neither State nor the Pentagon wanted Treasury making its own foreign policy judgments. They merely wanted Treasury cooperation, to the extent that it was necessary to carry out foreign policy.

Take the case of the Indonesian financial crisis in 1998. Treasury became increasingly dismissive of President Suharto's willingness and ability to implement economic reforms demanded by the IMF and eventually took the stance that any further large-scale aid to his regime would merely damage the fund's credibility. Seeking out his own foreign policy advice from the likes of Henry Kissinger, Paul Wolfowitz, Lee Kuan Yew, and others outside the government, Rubin infuriated the administration's foreign policy team by taking up the mantle of Indonesian political change. Rubin adviser Robert Boorstin, speaking of the prospects for successful economic reform in Indonesia, recalls writing memos saying that "as long as Suharto is in charge, this is going nowhere." The National Security Council's chief Asia specialist, Sandra Kristoff, said she was astounded at Rubin's insistence that economic reform would not work without political reform. "There were nearly fisticuffs in Erskine's office," she said, referring to White House Chief of Staff Erskine Bowles. Boorstin characterized the tussle this way: "They thought we were a bunch of ignoramuses poaching on their turf, and we thought they were willing to give any amount of money to anyone under the naïve assumption that it would actually stabilize the country."[8]

Mistakes were made on both sides. Stanley Roth, assistant secretary of state for East Asia, considered it preposterous that economic aid should be conditioned on political reform, as "Suharto will be here three years from now"—or so he thought.[9] As for Treasury, Rubin remembers "at the time of the South Korea crisis, being struck in discussion with a prominent New York banker by how little he and his company knew about a country to which they had extended a considerable amount of credit."[10] Yet this view is wholly inconsistent with Treasury's support for IMF conditionality on its Asian aid packages, which are now widely seen as having been almost comically interventionist on structural reform requirements. If major investors were truly ignorant about an Asian economy the size of Korea's, how is it that the requirements for reviving their confidence in Indonesia could extend to the dismantling of a clove monopoly?

Mistakes notwithstanding, there was much that was right in this process. Treasury's position, that evaluating prospects for successful economic reform required an informed judgment on Suharto's role in the political process, was surely correct. An informed economic judgment required an informed political judgment. Yet State's position, that whether Suharto should stay or go could hardly be decided on the basis of whether he could implement Treasury's economic reform agenda, was no less obviously correct. A political judgment could not be based solely on economic criteria.

The issue is therefore not which side has the monopoly on wisdom in the midst of a foreign financial crisis. The issue is whether the decision-making process can be improved.

It is tempting to believe that there must be an institutional fix for any imperfection in government decision making. Merge this, coordinate that, and all will be well. But we echo Charles Hill's warning to avoid "the temptation to react to any major governmental problem with a recommendation for structural or institutional remodeling."[11]

A foreign financial crisis does not always present the United States with a clearly defined problem. Where was the locus of the national interest in the Asia crisis? Was it fundamentally about politics or economics? Would the strategy be the same if approached from the perspective of protecting American security interests in a region dotted with potential flashpoints, such as the Korean peninsula and the Taiwan straits, as it would be if approached from the perspective of protecting American economic interests in a region which took 30 percent of U.S. exports? The political and economic questions, even taken in isolation, were extremely complex. In the case of Indonesia, should the political objective have been preventing regime change, managing it, or encouraging it? The proper answer may well depend on the timeframe: immediate regime change may not be desirable, but an orderly regime change a year hence may be. As for the economic objective, should it have been preventing widespread default or minimizing its impact domestically and abroad? And would the answer to this question be the same regardless of whether the strategy needed to implement it would make financial crises more likely or less manageable in the future?

Clearly, these are not easy questions. First and foremost, they involve setting priorities. Economic judgments must be made in the context of clearly articulated political priorities, and political judgments must be informed by an understanding of the likely consequences of pursuing or withholding economic intervention.

In establishing priorities, there is no bureaucratic alternative—merging this or coordinating that—to presidential judgment. President Clinton chose ultimately to rely on the judgment of his Treasury advisers, but there was no preordained hierarchy among Treasury, State, Defense, and the NSC. We suspect strongly that President Bush would have relied far more on his national security adviser than did President Clinton if faced with a currency-cum-political crisis in Indonesia.

During a foreign currency crisis, the president needs the best possible political and economic advice, but it cannot be left to the political and economic advisers each to establish their own mission. The president must define a single mission for which a coherent political and economic strategy is then crafted. How should political and economic perspectives be melded into a strategy?

It is clearly not sensible to create standby political and security expertise within Treasury relevant to dozens of potential crisis countries. It is, however, essential to infuse the foreign and security policy apparatus—State, Defense, and the NSC—with generalized expertise on the economics of currency crises. In a world in which significant crises are, regrettably, becoming about as frequent as leap year it is incumbent upon this group to develop its own economic literacy—not so that it can duplicate, or substitute for, the economic expertise in Treasury, but so its leaders have the capability independently to evaluate whether Treasury's economic judgment is consistent with political objectives.

This will require that the next generation of foreign policy and security experts have a considerably deeper background, cultivated in the market as well as in the classroom, in economics and finance. In a world in which financial flows have become such critical instruments in the development of national economies and political structures, the American foreign policy and security establishment simply must have the intellectual wherewithal to conduct financial statecraft.

How would this affect relations with Treasury? "We liked having people at the State Department we could talk to about these issues," Rubin told us.[12] He cited the example of former U.S. ambassador to Korea Stephen Bosworth, to whom he referred in his autobiography as "the kind of diplomat we're going to need more of in the future—one who combines foreign policy expertise and skill with a good understanding of economic issues."[13]

IMF Policy

If Washington isn't quite master of the IMF puppet, it is an open secret that it controls most of the strings during a crisis. Paradoxically, this may harm American foreign policy interests in the long run. If large Fund bailouts are more likely to be directed to key Washington allies, this may well induce risky overlending to precisely those countries for which Washington most fears the impact of default.

Although measuring moral hazard may be far more art than science, its presence in the case of Russia is simply undeniable: the anecdotal evidence of bankers betting on "too big to fail" logic is overwhelming (even if the bets ultimately failed). Former Treasury Undersecretary David Lipton recounted investors referring to Russian bonds at 80 percent yields as a "moral-hazard play."[14] Once the IMF had stepped in, it became impossible to restructure Russia's deadly short-term debt. A swap offer made to foreign investors by Goldman Sachs for the Russian government—give up your high-yielding ruble-denominated GKOs for lower-interest, long-term, dollar-denominated Eurobonds—was roundly rejected. It was trading "a bronco for a mule," according to one trader.[15]

In the cases of Mexico, Argentina, and Turkey the evidence of moral hazard bets may be less clear, but the evidence of U.S. foreign policy rather than internal Fund analysis driving intervention is not. Over time, it is only prudent to expect overlending to countries blessed to be a clear and present security concern for the United States. For this reason, it is imperative for Washington to implement policies now to restrain the compulsion, as well as the need, for large-scale crisis lending in the future.

The centerpiece of such policies must be international currency consolidation. The IMF's policy-setting Interim Committee, comprised of member nations' finance ministers and central bank governors, in 1997 recommended to the Executive Board that it amend the Fund's articles to "make the liberalization of capital movements one of the purposes of the Fund." Yet only by ridding the world of nontradable currencies will it be safe for capital flows. And capital flows will continue to grow robustly precisely because emerging economies want and need them, not because foreign financial institutions are able to force dollars upon them.

Whereas the domain of the dollar and the euro will continue to expand, and the world's stock of national currencies continue to decline, regardless of whether Washington or Brussels takes active steps to encourage it, this is clearly a long-term process. And in the long run there will be more than enough currency crises to bankrupt the IMF. Thus other major reforms will be necessary.

The IMF's current path involves three strategies. The first is to assist developing countries in implementing more effective independent monetary policy regimes, containing fiscal deficits, monitoring and controlling currency mismatches across the public and private sectors, and carrying out structural reforms aimed particularly at improving the safety and soundness of the banking sector. The second is to develop better warning signs of impending currency crises. And the third is to implement a form of international bankruptcy procedure, aimed at giving foreign creditors greater incentive to reach quick agreement on an orderly debt restructuring in the case of a crisis.

The first strategy, on its own, merely mimics the OECD's think-tank role, with free private consulting tacked on when discretion is required. This is a fairly harmless use of G-7 funds, provided that neither the G-7 nor its clients operate under any illusion that the IMF's economic advice has ever been systematically any better than that of the private think tanks that routinely criticize it.

Encouraging more fiscal transparency among client governments is a popular concomitant strategy, but is likely to be successful only with governments that have nothing worth hiding in the first place. Sinners rarely keep weblogs. The Thai government took active steps in 1997 to hide its financial position, selling dollars in the swaps market and pretending they were still usable as reserves.

"It would be close to impossible for a country to do what Thailand or South Korea or, earlier, Mexico did and hide its true reserve position," according to former Secretary Rubin.[16] We disagree. The use of sophisticated derivatives among governments will inevitably saturate the developing world, providing them with the same tools that rogue companies and governments in the rich world have used to disguise red ink. G-7 member Italy appears to have used swap contracts in the late 1990s much the way Enron did, to fudge its books. Yen-lira swaps struck at a seemingly bizarre exchange rate served artificially to lower the Italian budget deficit figure in the run-up to its fiscal qualification exam for eurozone membership.[17] In short, we cheer on the IMF and all others who encourage ever more prudent economic management in the developing world. At the same time, we harbor no illusions as to the perfectibility of IMF advice or the judgment and probity of the governments receiving it.

The second strategy, trying to improve crisis warning signs, is also well and good, provided the IMF keeps its doomsday guesses outside the earshot of private markets. Given the IMF's—indeed, everyone's—poor predictive record to date, the IMF is more apt to precipitate crises than prevent them by blaring default warning sirens on Wall Street.

The IMF has already backed off on the third strategy, creating an IMF "Chapter 11" for sovereigns, amidst withering criticism from both private lenders and public borrowers. The Sovereign Debt Restructuring Mechanism (SDRM) would create an IMF-sponsored forum to address crisis debt restructuring by bringing the borrower and its lenders together, disenfranchising individual litigants, and adjudicating claims on a global basis. Private lenders rightly object that the Chapter 11 analogy is misleading, albeit dangerously seductive. Among other things, SDRM would apply to already outstanding debt, thus nullifying existing contractual rights, while omitting the critical role of a bankruptcy trustee, who is normally charged with controlling a debtor's management and its assets during bankruptcy procedures.[18] Sovereigns, in turn, expect SDRM to frighten off their lenders entirely—an expectation actually considered one of its great attractions by supporters.[19] A more modest and sensible proposal gathering support is for the inclusion of voluntary collective action clauses (CACs) in sovereign debt contracts, which would prevent a small minority of bondholders from blocking a restructuring without subjecting the parties to a new form of supranational fiat in the event of a default.

Although these strategies are intended to reduce the demand for IMF crisis lending, they will not. The IMF's lending to the major emerging economies now exceeds its total lending at the peak of the Asian, Russian, and Brazilian crises, while its loan portfolio is also now in much more heavily indebted countries.[20] Its exposures are growing and are frighteningly undiversified. At the end of 2003, three countries, Brazil, Turkey, and Argentina, owed the IMF $67.5 billion, representing 72 percent of IMF outstanding general credit.[21]

The crisis portfolio will only expand further as capital account liberalization spreads currency mismatch across an ever-wider terrain. At best, new sovereign bankruptcy procedures will help speed up restructurings and thereby help prevent crises from spiraling, but they will not significantly mitigate the intense political pressure on the IMF to head off defaults with official lending. More important, international bonds were at the center of only one of the past eight emerging market currency crises. And in that one case, Argentina, more reserves were lost from a domestic bank run and a sharp contraction in international bank loans than from payments on maturing bonds.[22] Thus SDRMs and CACs address only a small part of the problem.

Moral hazard can, of course, be eliminated by simply ceasing such lending. Abolishing the IMF or downgrading it to a think tank would, however, only lead to political pressures to recreate a G-7 multilateral lending facility. These pressures would be particularly strong in the United States, as the IMF—official rhetoric notwithstanding—is a coveted tool for bailing out U.S. allies with European and Japanese funds. Furthermore, such political pressures would not be devoid of economic logic. Liquidity crises are frequently indistinguishable from solvency crises, but they are not the same, and efforts to keep the former from becoming the latter can be successful—as evidenced by Mexico in 1995.

Perhaps the best that can be hoped for politically is that the United States will come to see itself as Ulysses, best tied to the mast to hold forth against the siren's call for bailing out friendly insolvents. Limitations on the ability of IMF directors to approve lending unsupported by IMF staff analysis would go some way toward achieving this goal. Unsound IMF lending to Argentina over the period 2001–03 would at least have been considerably reduced in the absence of official U.S. support, whereas the United States could not have been blamed for withholding such support had the directors been unable to override the staff's much more critical economic judgment. Those who argue that such political self-abnegation is impossible would likely have said the same thing about independent central banks three decades ago—and they would have been wrong. An American administration crying, "Stop me before I lend again!" might even endear itself to Congress.

Just as diners expecting to split a restaurant bill will overorder, so IMF directors sharing the lending tab will overlend. Power reserved for the IMF managing director to reject lending unsupported by staff economic analysis would assist in enforcing stricter and more consistent criteria for IMF loans, thus ensuring more prudence and less moral hazard in such lending. It would not bar the United States or its G-7 allies from leading bailouts on their own, without IMF political cover or funds. The United States supplemented IMF lending with considerable bilateral funds in the cases of Mexico and Turkey. But it would place far more political constraints—legitimate, democratic constraints—on the use of bailout funds and oblige prospective G-7 lenders to clarify their criteria before their legislatures and the general public.

Dollarization as U.S. Foreign Policy

In the long term, finding ways of bribing people to dollarize, or at least give back the extra currency that is earned when dollarization takes place, ought to be an international priority. For the world as a whole, the advantage of dollarization seems clear to me.

—Lawrence Summers[23]

Dollarization Policy in the Clinton and Bush Administrations

Robert Rubin and Lawrence Summers held very different personal views on the merits of dollarization. Rubin thought little of it, and even less about it. Summers, in contrast, had been vocally supportive of dollarization prior to his political career, and quietly supportive once in it. The official administration position was strict neutrality: the United States would neither actively assist nor oppose the efforts of other nations to dollarize.

In testimony before the Senate Banking Committee in April 1999, Summers, then Rubin's deputy, identified the potential benefits of dollarization to the United States as cheaper and greater trade and capital flows with dollarizing countries, potentially greater stability and growth in these countries, and seigniorage revenues to the U.S. government. To this list, Treasury Assistant Secretary for International Affairs Edwin Truman added "the power and prestige that might be associated with a more international currency."[24] Summers identified potential costs as increased pressure from dollarized governments on the United States to make economic interventions on their behalf (perhaps to lower interest rates in a slowdown or to support their financial systems in a crisis) and possible resentment directed toward the United States by dollarized countries when U.S. monetary policy is seen as inappropriate and unresponsive to their needs.

In 2000, Republican Senator Connie Mack (FL) and Representative Paul Ryan (WI) introduced into the Senate and House, respectively, the International Monetary Stability Act, staking out an actively supportive stance on dollarization in the Republican-controlled legislature. The purpose of the act was to reduce the cost to foreign governments of dollarizing through the establishment of a formal, quantitative procedure to calculate seigniorage benefits to the United States and to rebate 85 percent of such benefits to dollarizing governments. The 15 percent differential was to be used to finance rebates to previously dollarized countries, to cover putative additional costs to the Fed of managing a larger money supply, and to leave a small profit for the Treasury.

The act would have neutralized one oft-repeated argument against dollarization—that it will result in significant lost seigniorage to dollarizing governments. In order to acquire the necessary dollar notes to dollarize a country, a dollarizing government would, operating without U.S. government support, have to furnish the Fed with interest-bearing dollar assets, such as Treasury securities, which the United States would otherwise have to pay interest on. As the loss of interest revenue to the foreign government represents a pure windfall to the United States, refunding it makes that government whole at no cost to the U.S. taxpayer.[25]

The findings in section 2 of the act emphasize the economic damage that monetary instability abroad has caused and identifies American encouragement of official dollarization as part of an ongoing U.S. effort "to strengthen the international financial architecture." The bill accords considerable leeway to the Treasury secretary to reduce or cancel seigniorage rebates in the event that recipient governments ceased to meet criteria established to ensure that they were legitimately dollarized, had opened their banking systems to foreign participation or met international banking standards,[26] and were cooperating with the United States in the prevention of money laundering and counterfeiting. The bill further stipulates that the remit of the Fed—with regard to monetary policy formulation and implementation, lender of last resort functions, and supervision of financial institutions—will not in any way be altered by countries adopting the dollar.

Despite his long-standing personal view that dollarization was a desirable development, Summers, then Treasury secretary, sent a letter to Senator Mack in July 2000 withholding administration support for the bill "at this time" on the grounds that a framework for sharing seigniorage "would raise a number of complex political, economic, [and] foreign policy issues, and U.S. budget issues." Treasury was concerned that a blanket seigniorage rebate scheme would give the appearance of being a massive new foreign aid program; something they were not anxious to launch in an election year. There were also concerns about details of the bill, such as how a future administration would deal with unfriendly foreign regimes that happened to rule dollarized countries with which America had taken on annual check-writing obligations.

The bill passed the Senate Banking Committee but was never considered in the full Senate owing to delays deriving from budget battles. In the House, the bill failed to pass out of the subcommittee, and Ryan failed to make progress with a revised version in July 2001.

The issue then lay politically dormant until a currency crisis hit the Dominican Republic in spring of 2004. The island it shares with politically fragile Haiti, whose president had only recently been deposed, could ill afford the political and social turmoil that threatened with soaring inflation. The crisis revived interest in dollarization in Congress, to which Bush Treasury Undersecretary for International Affairs John Taylor was obliged to respond. Taylor stated in testimony that the dollarization programs in El Salvador and Ecuador were "very positive developments for those countries" and that the administration would be "very supportive of that approach" if the Dominicans chose to do the same, pledging technical assistance.[27]

Where to Go from Here

Money has always been an instrument of foreign policy—not merely a means of influencing individuals, but entire societies.

The destabilization of enemy money has been a staple of warfare for hundreds of years. The Milanese duke Galeazzo Sforza counterfeited Venetian currency in 1470 to undermine the economy of his enemies in Venice. The British began counterfeiting colonial American currencies in 1775 to undermine the American rebellion. Germany counterfeited an astounding $7 billion, at today's value, of British pounds during the Second World War in an attempt to damage the British economy. The United States even counterfeited Cuban pesos during the Bay of Pigs invasion in 1961.[28]

Destabilizing a nation's money unsettles its political and legal structures and undermines the state's ability to maintain internal order and security against external threats. Stabilizing a nation's money, on the other hand, can have a mirror-image effect: promoting social cohesiveness, buttressing the rule of law, and bringing credibility and consistency to foreign policy.

Yet it matters not one iota whether that money is manufactured or managed domestically. The British government has appointed foreigners to its Monetary Policy Committee, albeit with a wholly British domestic remit. The French government has gone much further, ceding all monetary authority to a European Central Bank in Frankfurt, run by independent appointees from throughout Europe pledged to act in the interests of the twelve-nation eurozone as a whole. And, critically, the French government ceded such powers with clear *political* motivations: to enhance the security of the French state and its influence in world affairs. In central America, Ecuador in 2000 and El Salvador in 2001 relinquished the prerogative to impose a national money even without sharing in the control of the money to be used within their borders, dollarizing their economies, as Panama did a century ago, and Guatemala and Nicaragua are seriously considering the option. It is clearly in America's national interest to support this trend.

Of the benefits of dollarization to the United States which Summers cited in his April 1999 testimony, stability is the one with the most profound implications. Currency crises abroad increasingly affect living standards at home. The largest American financial institutions are heavily exposed to foreign exchange risk in the developing world, and a series of large blows to their balance sheets could lead to damaging domestic retrenchment and insolvencies. Trade and investment flows are dramatically disrupted when currencies collapse, undermining business investment and employment. And whereas dollarization will not itself turn enemies into friends or conflict into cooperation, the elimination of currency crises will go a long way toward preventing the sudden and dire collapses in economic and social conditions that give rise to security threats. Left and right of the American political spectrum should therefore be united in wishing to harness globalization to dollarization.

The proposed International Monetary Stability Act needs to be revived. The concerns laid out in the July 2000 Summers letter notwithstanding, the *actual* "political, economic, foreign policy and budget issues" involved in repeated U.S. (and U.S.-led IMF) bailouts of allies with collapsed currencies over the past decade should have been far more worrisome. These interventions put tens of billions of U.S. taxpayer dollars at direct risk, while the conditions imposed ostensibly to limit default risk frequently strained U.S. relations with crisis governments severely. Presidential discretion to suspend seigniorage rebates owing to national security concerns can and should be accommodated in the act, but failure to pass it only makes such concerns more likely to materialize.

The degree to which the United States should stand ready to provide emergency lending to dollarized countries would be a particularly contentious issue. Governments in dollarized countries cannot respond to short-term financial problems, such as bank liquidity shortfalls, by printing money and may therefore want assurances of future assistance from the United States.

Although American promises to provide large-scale, uncollateralized emergency lending facilities are as imprudent as they are politically impracticable, an explicit acknowledgment that discretionary lending may be in the national interest is the only honest and sensible way to address the issue. After all, this would do no more than ratify the propriety of past American actions when allies faced financial crisis, such as recourse to $20 billion from the Exchange Stabilization Fund and Federal Reserve swap network in the case of Mexico in 1994. The only difference is that with devaluation risk eliminated, both the likelihood and severity of any future liquidity crisis in a dollarized country will be dramatically reduced.

The Role of U.S. Dollar Policy

The proposition that dollarization will stabilize economies, eliminate currency crises, promote safe capital flows, and reduce antiglobalization sentiment is founded on the assumption that the United States will pursue economic policies over the long run that serve to underpin the dollar as an international store of value. This is perhaps the most compelling intellectual case for the doctrine, made famous in its repetition by Robert Rubin, that "a strong dollar is in America's national interest."

What policies will give confidence to people around the world that the dollar is an asset worth holding over time? In other words, what policies will serve to ensure that the dollar will maintain its value vis-à-vis other savings vehicles, such as euros or gold?

At the macroeconomic level, the answer is, first and foremost, controlling the size of the national debt. At some point, persistent large government budget deficits, which contribute to current account deficits, must raise questions among foreign holders of dollar assets about the ability of the American government to service its debt without economically damaging tax increases or engineered inflation. Is there reason to be concerned now?

In 1985, when the U.S. current account deficit stood at 2.8 percent of GDP, foreign governments owned 8.4 percent of U.S. government debt outstanding. In 2004, with the current account deficit at 5.7 percent of GDP, foreign governments owned a much higher 27.6% of the total debt outstanding (see figure 3). This is a cause for concern, both because it represents a greater concentration of holdings and because noneconomic factors are more likely to be relevant among state actors.

Consider the dangers of the greater concentration of dollar-asset holdings among national central banks, a group highly prone to herding. In the 1990s, central banks around the world reacted to a sustained decline in the price of gold by selling massive amounts from their reserves. Over the course of the 1980s, when the gold price fell from $615 to $381 an ounce, central banks *added* a net 344 tons of gold to their reserves. Yet over the 1990s, as gold fell further to $279, central banks sold a net 3,148 tons. In one year alone, 1992, central bank sales amounted to nearly a quarter of the annual gold supply, depressing the price by an estimated 8.27%. Central bank net gold sales continued at an annual rate of 500 tons in the early years of this decade.[30]

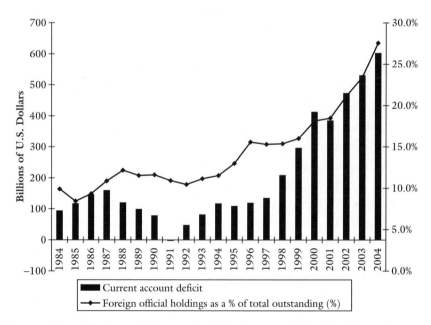

Figure 3. The U.S. Current Account Deficit and Foreign Official Holdings of U.S. Treasury Securities. Source: U.S. Department of the Treasury; International Monetary Fund; Bureau of Economic Analysis.[29]

The dollar has fully supplanted gold as the foundation of the world's monetary system. But between 2001 and the end of 2004 the dollar lost a third of its value against the euro, the currency next in line for such a role. Should the dollar continue an extended decline, under pressure from persistently high current account deficits, there is every reason to believe that central banks will seek greater diversification in their reserves, most likely into euros. As central banks bailed out of gold in the 1990s, their herding out of dollars would accelerate the dollar's decline, threatening its status as the world's standard denominator of value. Indeed, signs of such a possibility were clear in late 2004, with reports of dollar sales by the Chinese and Russian central banks, said to be for euros and Asian currencies, and strong hints of curtailing future Treasury purchases from Japan, Korea, and India.[31]

Entering 2005, the Bush administration appeared to be wholly unconcerned by the dollar's decline, seeing it instead as a natural and healthy mechanism to reverse the U.S. trade deficit. However, the latest econometrics evidence shows U.S. imports to be highly impervious to exchange rate changes and casts grave doubt on this benign view of the currency market's role in curing the country's persistent and growing structural trade imbalance.[32] This points to an urgent need for the United States to reduce its annual budget deficits substantially. Roughly one-third of the decline in national saving produced by an increase in the budget deficit is financed by capital from abroad.[33] America is currently importing about $2 billion of foreign capital a day. As policy initiatives to motivate an increase in private saving have failed over many decades, the only safe, effective, and responsible way for the country to reduce its external deficit is to raise public savings, meaning to cut the budget deficit. If, instead, the Bush administration continues to project an image of insouciance over the fate of the dollar, this will undermine the currency's hard-earned role as the world's preeminent standard of value, reduce America's influence over the setting of global norms in international commerce, and undermine the further march of dollarization.

Why a "Currency of the Americas" Is in No One's Interest

The reason dollarization is attractive abroad is precisely because the U.S. Federal Reserve has established a hard-won reputation for maintaining stable dollar prices over the past quarter century. To reconstitute its decision-making apparatus in order to embrace "other perspectives" can only serve to undermine confidence in the dollar regime, which is the essence of the decision to dollarize in the first place. At some point in the future, it may well be within the bounds of both political and market acceptability to add non-Americans to the Board of Governors with a remit to consider dollar price stability beyond America's borders. In essence, the dollar could morph into something more akin to the multinational euro.

Yet it is in no one's interest to create doubt as to the Fed's low-inflation commitment, particularly given the softness of its legislative underpinning. The 1978 Full Employment and Balanced Growth Act, known popularly as the Humphrey-Hawkins Act, regrettably muddied the Fed's statutory allegiance to stable prices by committing it simultaneously to "maximum employment," a goal few reputable economists any longer see as justifying policies targeted at anything other than low inflation. Whereas inflation hawks Paul Volcker and Alan Greenspan felt unconstrained by the "maximum employment" objective, markets would punish the dollar brutally if future Fed boards were to create uncertainty in this area. A wise Congress would therefore underpin the growing internationalization of the dollar by legislating the Fed's unitary commitment to stable prices.

The Limits of Dollarization

Dollarization, as a matter of economics, is clearly not the best option for the entire globe. But countries adopting one of the handful of internationally traded reserve currencies, such as the euro, is manifestly in the economic interest of their populations as well as those of their trading partners. How should the United States most effectively promote this process?

To address this question sensibly, America's own self-interest must first be understood. Clearly, supplanting the world's currencies with the dollar would serve America's interests on many fronts. Global trade and investment flows would expand dramatically, and currency crises would become a virtual oxymoron. In short, assuming (as economists are wont to do) an enlightened American monetary policy, America and the world would be richer, and more durably so through time. Then there are the political intangibles of the power and prestige projected through a global American currency. Assuming (again) an enlightened diplomacy, dollarization should ultimately result in a greater willingness of other nations to participate in a rules-based system of international economic and political relations—a system which America did much to establish after the Second World War.

But global dollarization is obviously not in the cards. Political resistance to adopting American monetary policy will, quite naturally, be an insurmountable obstacle throughout much of the world. Furthermore, the patterns of trade, investment, and labor migration flows will, as a matter of economics, frequently favor the adoption of other currencies. Central and eastern European countries, for example, would more logically adopt the euro.

The situation in Asia is more complex. Economic criteria currently favor the yen in parts of the region, but the rapid rise of China as an economic force will change this calculus over time. Political realities, however, will ensure that no country in the region abandons its currency for either the yen or the renminbi. Yet while the day is likely two decades off, the creation of a multinational Asian currency, fashioned on the back of political reconciliation among Japan, China, and Korea, is a strong possibility, particularly if the euro moves successfully into adolescence. The idea has already been a major topic of discussion in regional forums, such as the 2004 annual meeting of the Asian Development Bank. Such a union would likely be built by or within the ten-member Association of Southeast Asian Nations (ASEAN)[34] or the so-called ASEAN+3 (which would add China, Japan, and South Korea).

Even in the slow-changing Middle East, the issue of currency consolidation is now a topic of open high-level discussion. The Gulf Cooperation Council, a customs union comprising Saudi Arabia, Bahrain, Kuwait, Oman, Qatar, and the United Arab Emirates, envisions a monetary union with a common currency by 2010. While the timetable may be overly ambitious, the goal is significant in its statement, as a recognition of the benefits of monetary denationalization and currency consolidation.

What then is an optimistic yet realistic goal for American financial statecraft? Dollarization of Central America, and possibly of wider Latin America, clearly fits the bill. Mexican public opinion polls in 1998 and

1999 showed support for dollarization in the 80–90 percent range. Canada too could one day join a dollar bloc, which would provide a significant economic boost to a future Free Trade Area of the Americas. With over 80 percent of its exports destined for the United States, Canada is more deeply integrated with the American economy than is Switzerland with Europe. In fact, no euro country has a higher share of its exports destined for the eurozone.[35]

Dollarization is clearly not amenable to a hard sell from Washington. National governments must come to see it as being in their, and their people's, economic interest, and public efforts by Washington to persuade them of its merits are bound to backfire. Yet a standing offer of technical assistance and seigniorage rebates, as envisioned in the International Monetary Stability Act of 2000, would clearly assist other governments in building their own cases for domestic public support.

Euroization of Europe to, and perhaps eventually beyond, Russia's borders might seem to clash with an American dollarization drive, but as a practical matter it would complement it. The central and eastern European economies are better off euro-based, and their prosperity can only be an economic and political plus for the United States. Provided America continues to control inflation effectively and does not let its current fiscal profligacy get out of hand, this would not pose a challenge to the dollar's dominant international role. Washington should therefore be supportive of euroization. The big question is whether Brussels will be.

Euroization

Official American neutrality on dollarization illustrates an unfortunate inertia in Treasury's conduct of international monetary affairs. Official EU *hostility* to euroization, on the other hand, illustrates an almost pathological insularity in the Franco-German-led drive for European integration. Indeed, it is difficult to imagine a matter on which the official EU stance is more antithetical to the interests of its most ardent supporters.

Although non-EU members Kosovo and Montenegro have euroized unilaterally, with neither assistance nor obstruction from the EU, the European Council of Ministers and the European Commission have stated clearly and repeatedly that such action is undesirable and, indeed, impermissible. According to one council document, "It should be made clear that any unilateral adoption of the single currency by means of 'euroisation' would run counter to the underlying economic reasoning of [European Monetary Union] in the Treaty, which foresees the eventual adoption of the euro as the endpoint of a structured convergence process within a multilateral framework. Therefore, unilateral 'euroisation' would not be a way to circumvent the stages foreseen by the Treaty for the adoption of the euro."[36]

As a matter of economics, this statement is illogical. As a matter of legality, it is dubious. And as a matter of political principle, it is foolish.

In explaining why non-eurozone members "cannot" adopt the euro unilaterally, the European Commission says that "the credibility of the euro rests on the economic fundamentals of the Member States belonging to the euro zone, which participate fully in the institutions defining the monetary policy and the co-ordination of the economic policies of members."[37] Yet since non-eurozone members do not participate in any eurozone policymaking institutions, they are not in a position to undermine the currency's "credibility" by using it. Indeed, they are hardly in a position even to affect its internal or external value in any meaningful way: all the May 2004 EU accession countries combined, for example, account for only about 6 percent of eurozone GDP.[38] In contrast, euroization can be of tremendous benefit to the euroizing countries themselves. Estonia, for example, adopted a deutschmark-based currency board in 1992, which subsequently morphed into a euro-based board when the mark was eliminated. Speculative attacks on the board during the Asian and Russian currency crises led to damaging interest rate spikes, such as the surge from 8 percent to 19 percent in 1998, which would have been avoided entirely had the country euroized outright.[39]

Legally, the commission holds to the view that a country euroizing unilaterally would be in violation of the sequencing set out in the Treaty of Amsterdam for accession to the single currency. Yet this sequencing assumes that participation in eurozone institutions goes hand in hand with replacement of the national currency by the euro, whereas unilateral euroizers will simply have no national currency to replace at the time they are considered for the final stage (stage 3) of eurozone accession. Telling a government that it cannot eliminate its own national currency is clearly not a prerogative of any EU body.

Of course, EU threats of political or economic retaliation may discourage a government from euroizing, but to do so would be to fight a war that is already won. The reason that fiscal, inflation, and exchange rate criteria for eurozone participation were originally established (in the Maastricht Treaty) was to ensure market credibility for the new currency. But just as the internationalization of the dollar is a reflection of, and not a threat to, the credibility of the dollar, the internationalization of the euro can only be of benefit to the EU at this point. Witness the currency market's nonchalance in the face of France's and Germany's flouting of the 3 percent deficit-to-GDP ceiling in 2003—the clearest possible indication that the market has little fear that the European Central Bank will try to inflate away member-state debt. Surely, at this stage, the spread of the euro beyond the borders of the EU can only increase the confidence vested in it by private investors and central banks around the globe.

We assume that the EU will always do the right thing, at least after exhausting every other option. So it is only a matter of time now before its political leaders come to see that assisting, rather than opposing, euroization is in the EU's strong self-interest. It will increase trade and investment flows among an expanding number of euroized nations. It will increase the role of the euro as an international reserve currency. It will reduce the risk of de-euroization by EU member states in the future. And it will contribute to the creation of a durable European political identity which, after all, was the driving force behind European monetary union in the first place.

When the day of Europe's epiphany arrives, Turkey should be the first beneficiary. An official EU offer to accommodate Turkish euroization—with technical assistance and a seigniorage rebate—would mark a major milestone in Europe's hesitant embrace of its Muslim neighbor, in Turkey's permanent economic stabilization, and in laying the foundations of a world finally safe for financial globalization.

8

THE FUTURE OF FINANCIAL STATECRAFT

Notwithstanding two decades of debate over whether political speed bumps should be raised in the international marketplace for capital, the trend to date has been clear. Policymakers in the developed and, increasingly, the developing world have reached the conclusion that the economic benefits of allowing capital to flow cross-border from suppliers to users outweigh the costs of maintaining or erecting barriers to stop it. This is clearly illustrated in the trade figures displayed in chapter 1, which show that, since the mid-1980s, trade in securities has grown dramatically relative to traditional trade in goods and services. Yet whereas there is as yet no serious political movement afoot anywhere to reverse this trend, we have in the United States clearly witnessed a growth in efforts both to *accelerate* it generally and, simultaneously, to *constrain* specific cross-border capital movements for political purposes.

Financial statecraft, we have argued, is becoming an increasingly significant political phenomenon with potentially important economic and political implications. The two parts of this book express very different sentiments on the prospects for financial statecraft in the American diplomatic arsenal. Consistent with our view that financial markets are powerful vehicles for expanding prosperity as well as tremendously adaptable in the face of efforts to direct them (whether for good or for ill), we are, when looking out to the future of financial statecraft, macro-enthusiasts and micro-skeptics. On the one hand, we believe that far more fundamental reforms can and should be undertaken to make capital flows from the northern to the southern hemisphere as safe and productive as capital flows from the east to the west coast of the United States. And there are serious consequences to not undertaking such reforms. On the other hand, we believe that the growing enthusiasm for fighting foreign evils— from terrorism to weapons proliferation to human rights abuses— through bank and stock exchange regulation needs to be nipped in the bud. The emerging vanguard of economic warriors overstates both the importance of money to their foreign policy aims as well as our capacity to control its movements.

We conclude with a forward-looking tour of the terrain we have covered in this book; starting with banking regulation, traversing the realm of securities trading, and closing with the big picture on global capital flows.

The past three decades have witnessed the growing internationalization of banking, with the American government seeking both to advance the process and to restrict its parameters. One consistent goal since the LDC debt crisis of the early 1980s has been to restrain American banks from "overlending" while simultaneously protecting them from the competition of foreign banks that might. The holy grail of a level playing field in international banking is, however, a chimera, as governments will continue to find ways to support the operations of favored national institutions. (France and Italy, for example, continue to push for the creation of "national champion" megabanks while blocking foreign takeovers.) But the United States, operating through the G-10 Basel Committee on Banking Supervision, can and should do a better job in harnessing market forces to compel internationally active banks to operate with sufficient capital, such that they can absorb significant market shocks without recourse to moral hazard–inducing government bailouts. Obliging such banks to issue credibly unsecured subordinated debt, and bonding regulatory interventions to falls in the market price of such debt, is a far more promising approach than the complex and arbitrageable Basel framework which took root in 1988.

Stopping cross-border financial flows related to drug trafficking, terrorism, weapons proliferation, and other activities harmful to America's national interests will be a far more complex task and, unfortunately but inevitably, will yield fewer tangible results.

To have even a modicum of success, America must engage, in spirit and deed as well as in words, dozens of other countries whose financial institutions are or could be used as conduits for targeted funds. Acting with insufficient foreign cooperation may be not only ineffective but counterproductive, as it may encourage financial activities that would otherwise have taken place within America's legal jurisdiction to move outside it. The capital markets of the developed nations have become so interchangeable that arbitraging rules across borders has become second nature to sophisticated participants. Even the most well-intentioned regulations—such as those emanating from the Sarbanes-Oxley legislation, designed to improve corporate governance in the wake of the Enron and WorldCom implosions—have had the effect of deterring capital raising on American securities exchanges. Multilateralism has become a prerequisite for success—not because America needs permission to act, but because money, by its very nature in our digitized world, flows across legal borders with such ease as to make America's physical border with Mexico appear, in comparison, almost impermeable. And there is no substitute for old-fashioned, forceful and energetic diplomacy in bringing about the cooperation of others.

Moreover, it is exceptionally difficult to use the financial markets to control the activities of those who are not driven by the profit motive, and it gets ever more difficult as the cost of their targeted activities falls. The cost to terrorists of carrying out virtually every heinous act they can think of is in steep decline, and in many cases already low, given that the necessary conventional, chemical, biological, and nuclear tools and know-how to produce them are becoming ever more abundant around the globe.

"Economic warfare" is a phrase now bandied about with great enthusiasm in Washington, as it implies that America has the capability of punishing her enemies effectively with little effort and no loss of life. Capital markets sanctions have become the centerpiece of coercive financial statecraft. Frequently the agendas are multiple, such as when the stated foreign policy target is a genocidal regime in Sudan while the sanctions target is a Chinese oil company. But as we have yet to see a case in which either companies or regimes were moved to behave in the way supporters of capital markets sanctions wished them to, it is clearly time to rethink the role of such sanctions in the foreign policy arsenal. Even when motivated by noble ambitions, applying toy gun tactics can mislead both responsible policymakers and the wider public that America is doing something meaningful when it is not, undermine America's diplomatic credibility abroad, and produce significant collateral economic damage by driving financial activities outside the scope of America's legal jurisdiction.

In evaluating the effectiveness of financial sanctions it is critical to distinguish clearly between the ability to inflict economic harm, the ability to influence a target's behavior, and the ability to achieve actual foreign policy aims. In the cases of the capital markets sanctions campaigns against Gazprom, PetroChina, and Talisman the results were not encouraging. The economic harm inflicted was small or negligible. The impact on the behavior of the targets worked *against* U.S. interests, in that these companies—and many others which observed the campaigns, such as Lukoil—drew the lesson that it is frequently best to raise international capital outside the SEC's jurisdiction, rather than the lesson that the sanctions supporters wished them to draw, which was that companies should not do business in countries designated off limits by the American Congress. Finally, and most significantly, there was no advancement of U.S. foreign policy aims. The targeted firms continued to pursue their targeted business activities, and the targeted governments at the end of the chain—in these cases, Iran and Sudan—failed to change their policies.

Does this mean that financial sanctions against nonstate actors can never achieve foreign policy aims? No, but the hurdles are extremely high. First, the United States must impose controls on a residency basis, rather than a situs basis: that is, U.S. citizens and companies must be enjoined from committing funds to a targeted entity, rather than the entity being enjoined from raising funds "in the United States." An entity barred from listing on the NYSE can simply list in London or Hong Kong and access U.S. capital with great ease. This sanctions strategy can, it must be noted, impose very significant costs on U.S. investors if their holdings are already large and they are obliged to divest, particularly in haste. Second, this strategy must be duplicated across a number of countries with developed capital markets, such as the United Kingdom, France, Germany, Switzerland, and Japan. In the cases of Gazprom and

PetroChina, we should point out, such an outcome would have been unthinkable. None of those countries would have cooperated. Third, assuming that the sanctions succeed in deterring the targeted company from doing business in the targeted country, its government must be unable to find suitable alternative suppliers. Again, in the cases of Gazprom and PetroChina, many companies could have performed their roles and done so without requiring access to U.S. capital. Finally, the products or services being sought by the targeted country must be of such importance that its government would rather capitulate to U.S. demands than simply go without. All in all, this is a pretty tall order for financial sanctions.

While debate rages on about the wisdom of allowing unrestricted capital flows into and out of developing countries, capital flows themselves will rage on. Governments and businesses in developing countries need capital to fund investments. They raise capital in dollars because dollars have come to be accepted as international money, and capital abroad is vastly more abundant than capital at home. (Imagine if Microsoft and Amazon.com had been restricted to raising capital from Washington state residents because of capital flow restrictions between Washington and the rest of the United States.)

But a national economy with large debts in dollars and assets in money that is not accepted outside the country is a dangerous mix. Dollar debts that are manageable at a given exchange rate can quickly become unmanageable if selling pressure moves the rate against the local currency. Even countries without significant dollar debt can be at risk. When banks in developing countries get into difficulty, citizens flock to dollars in order to protect their savings. It doesn't matter whether the government guarantees their deposits, as the citizens frequently fear inflation and devaluation more than they fear the actual loss of their deposits. A currency crisis can therefore be triggered *even where currency itself has nothing to do with a country's financial difficulties.*

Some countries do try to stop their citizens from buying or holding dollars, but it is a misnomer to characterize such countries as developing. Invariably they are not. There will be fewer and fewer such countries as time passes. The only serious policy question regarding capital flows to LDCs is therefore how to accommodate them safely.

Some countries, like Chile, implement regulations to raise the cost to foreign capital suppliers of withdrawing money quickly. Others, like South Korea, build up a war chest of dollar reserves. Both strategies entail a very real cost, and neither eliminates the risk. Economists at the IMF and elsewhere offer advice on beefing up bank risk management and supervision, but a fragile banking sector is at least as much a *result* of dangerous currency mismatch as it is a cause of financial crises.

The LDC debt crisis of the early 1980s marked the emergence of capital flows as an economic phenomenon meriting the political attention previously reserved for trade flows, and much more. It marked an epochal transition from the "age of the current account" to the "age of the capital account," with capital flows taking on rapidly growing geopolitical significance. As we saw in chapter 5, foreign financial crises produce American security problems. Yet American financial statecraft has yet to adapt effectively.

The Mexican, Asian, and Russian crises during the two Clinton administrations brought home just how intimately economics and foreign policy have become interwoven. Geoeconomics has emerged as a policy area in its own right. Its growing importance will require that the next generation of American foreign and security policy analysts have the experience and intellectual wherewithal to make sense of the way in which economic and financial market forces are acting to reshape the diplomatic landscape, while both constraining some strategic options and expanding others.

Thinking and policies need to change. These are the areas we have highlighted.

First, the United States should ignore pleas from its financial services sector and stop demanding capital account liberalization in countries with which it negotiates free trade agreements. Premature capital account liberalization has been a disaster for some LDCs. Arguing for "national treatment" to be accorded American financial services firms is fine and proper, but many LDCs simply do not have the capacity to prevent dangerous currency mismatches from infusing their economies once capital flows are fully liberalized. Future American governments faced with governments abroad and banks at home crying for multibillion dollar bailouts may rue inheriting what their predecessors bargained so hard for.

Second, the United States should lead a G-7 effort to depoliticize IMF decision making, in its own long-term interests. The evidence from both scholarly studies and accounts of former IMF officials is overwhelming: when U.S. foreign policy interests come into play, the IMF is fundamentally incapable of getting its clients to make the policy reforms that would make future loans unnecessary.[1] Although IMF economic assessments may be far from perfect, IMF conditionality would certainly be far more credible and effective if the behavior of governments seeking and receiving massive loans were not distorted by knowledge that American officials would simply override the conditions later.

Abolishing the IMF, or its lending desk, however, would accomplish nothing positive. Some financial crises are legitimately liquidity crises, and eliminating a multilateral lending facility would therefore risk turning many of them into solvency crises. Furthermore, the political pressures to recreate a G-7 lending facility would be so great that we would merely wind up reestablishing the IMF with a different logo. The key reform is therefore to ban, as a matter of stated IMF policy, political lending, or lending unsupported by the economic analysis of the IMF managing director and his staff.

The long-term answer, however, is to rid the world of unwanted currencies. Having a national money is not only becoming less and less useful as the world becomes more and more interconnected economically and financially, but it is becoming more and more destabilizing. Collapsed currencies leave poverty, fear, anger, and insecurity in their wake. National monies have become the Achilles' Heel of globalization. The Asian, Russian, and Latin American currency crises not only immiserated millions in the affected countries, but created or exacerbated significant security threats for the United States.

The recent unilateral adoption of the dollar in Ecuador and El Salvador and of the euro in Kosovo and Montenegro can and should presage a global denationalization of money. In the case of Latin America and the Balkans, governments ditching their national currencies would represent no more than an accommodation of ever more deeply entrenched local practices: saving in a trusted external money, concluding contracts in such a money, and measuring value in it. The United States has a compelling national interest in dollarization beyond its borders and needs to resurrect the enlightened efforts of the 106th Congress to accommodate and assist it. Even more urgently, it must reverse its present course of fiscal profligacy and insouciance toward the fate of the dollar. If the Bush administration does not move credibly and robustly to reverse the worrying long-term budget deficit trend, it will undermine global confidence in the dollar as a store of value and stop dollarization dead in its tracks. The fact that neither the euro nor any other currency is yet in a position to step into the dollar's global role should provide no consolation. A setback to dollarization means a setback on the path to currency consolidation generally, with all that implies for further crises and more antiglobalization sentiment. And as Martin Wolf has so persuasively argued, "The world needs more globalization, not less."[2]

An enlightened American financial statecraft will always be consistent with this principle. America's long-term prosperity and security are intimately bound up with a liberal, rules-based international economic and political order to which people around the globe aspire to be attached. Given the nature of money and securities in the digital age, financial markets are an exceptionally important part of that order. They adapt to and arbitrage rules across jurisdictions in ways and at speeds which policymakers too often fail to appreciate fully. It has been our aim in this book to further this appreciation in the service of promoting a wiser and more effective financial statecraft in the future.

NOTES

Chapter 1. What Is Financial Statecraft?

1. The parenthetical definitions are ours.
2. See Baldwin (1985:30).
3. This distinction is consistent with the understanding of "foreign economic policy" applied, for example, by Benjamin Cohen (1968) and Robert Pastor (1980).
4. See O'Sullivan (2003:12).
5. See ibid. (2003:300). Other notable sanctions texts include Hufbauer et al. (1990), Elliot et al. (forthcoming), and Haass (1998).
6. See Cronin (1999).

Chapter 2. Banking and Foreign Policy

1. See Baumol (2003).
2. The National Bank Act was revolutionary in another respect. Until 1863, except for two twenty-year periods when the federal government chartered a single bank (the First and Second National Banks of the United States), banks received their charters only from the states. At the time the Civil War broke out, there over 7,000 such banks, each with its own bank notes, which were used with great difficulty in locales outside the states (and cities) where the banks actually were located. To help assure that citizens would use only one currency, the National Bank Act also placed a tax on note issues by state banks.
3. See Perry (1975:2223).
4. See Cohen (1981:7, 32).
5. See Spiro (1999:57).
6. Then-Secretary of the Treasury William Simon negotiated a secret arrangement so that the Saudi central bank bought U.S. Treasuries outside of the government's normal auction process. See Spiro (1999:x).
7. See Seidman (1989:38).

8. The conventional wisdom that the banks loaned money to those LDCs that needed it most, i.e., net oil importers, may not be accurate. For a comprehensive statistical analysis of bank lending at the time, see Spiro (1999). Spiro documents that there is "not much correlation" between bank credits and the extent to which countries were net oil importers. Instead, while recycling occurred, it was carried out largely through aid provided by industrialized country governments and to a lesser extent from OPEC nations.

9. See Cohen (1986:208).

10. See U.S. Senate Committee on Foreign Relations, Subcommittee on Foreign Relations (1977:5).

11. See Burns (1977).

12. See Seidman (1989:38).

13. Prior to that time, oil prices had been inching up as OPEC members continued to exercise their newfound ability to set world oil prices. But OPEC alone was not responsible for the price jump in 1979. Oil companies and oil purchasers, worried that the Iranian revolution might trigger further instability in the Middle East and thus the threat of another oil embargo or production cutback, rushed to fill their inventories. This panic buying only made the higher prices that buyers feared a self-fulfilling prophecy.

14. Quoted in Grant (1980:7).

15. See Wallich (1981:8–14).

16. See *Wall Street Journal* (1981).

17. Wriston's well-known opinion (1982) that countries will always "own [in resources and production capability] more than they owe," and thus are fundamentally different from businesses, is cited frequently.

18. Quoted in Greider (1987:436). Taken as a whole, LDC debtor countries saw their GDP decline by an average of 1 percent in 1981, 2.5 percent in 1982, and a staggering 4.8 percent in 1983. See Sachs (1986:400).

19. Moreover, at least in principle, regulators oversee banks' accounting, trying to ensure that loans in particular are properly accounted for and that banks set aside sufficient reserves to cover their likely losses on loans.

20. The guideline ratios at the time were 6 percent for smaller banks and 5.5 percent for regional and large banks. Importantly, the 17 largest multinational banks were specifically exempted—not only would they have been unable to meet the guidelines, the reasoning went, but pressuring them to raise capital or reduce lending during a recession could make the downturn even worse.

21. Volcker is quoted to this effect in Greider (1987: 439–40).

22. Cited in Steil (1994).

23. See Cooper and Little (2001:16–23).

24. See Peek (1999:1).

25. The 1988 Basel Accord covered all international banks in the member countries. The United States went further, imposing the rules on *all* its banks, alongside the preexisting leverage ratios that had been imposed in 1985.

26. For a similar critique of the Basel standards, see Tarullo (forthcoming).

27. There has been much debate about the true impact of Basel's risk-weighting system on bank lending. See Hall (1993). Of course, to some extent, banks were purchasing Treasuries because of a drop in loan demand during the 1991–92 recession. But the magnitude of the banks' increased purchases of Treasuries suggests that the bias toward purchasing government bonds built into the Basel system also played an important role in discouraging banks from making loans and prompting them to buy U.S. government bonds instead.

28. Tier 1 capital is composed of shareholders' equity and retained earnings.

29. As two researchers concluded for the National Bureau of Economic Research, "The non-performing loan problem [in Japan] that surfaced in the 1990s was a direct result of the financial sector's excessive exposure to real estate in the later 1980s." See Dinc and McGuire (2003).

30. European bank regulators had similar fears about some of their insolvent banks in the 1980s and 1990s.

31. Countries can still deny licenses to foreign banks that do not meet the standards, which in fact U.S. regulators have done.

32. For an excellent guide, see Tarullo (forthcoming). For an even more critical view, see Shadow Financial Regulatory Committee (2000).

33. See Tarullo (forthcoming).

34. The system of prompt corrective action was developed by two well-respected financial economists during the 1980s, who urged that banks maintain even higher capital ratios than those that regulators eventually adopted. See Benston and Kauffman (1988).

35. See Estrella (2004:1469–98) and Furfine (1999:33–56).

36. The Basel agreement also requires banks to hold capital against some fraction of their off-balance sheet liabilities, such as guarantees that are not recorded on the balance sheet. A subordinated debt requirement expressed as a minimum percentage of total assets could also easily use the same adjustment for off-balance items that is already part of the existing Basel provisions. We would limit the subordinated debt requirement to banking organizations above a certain asset size threshold (consolidating the assets of different banks belonging to a common holding company to prevent banking organizations from circumventing the requirement by splitting themselves up) because smaller banks cannot sell such small amounts of subordinated debt at reasonable cost, nor is the market for such debt yet sufficiently developed to absorb debt issues by smaller institutions.

37. We are not the first to recommend a subordinated debt requirement. The idea was suggested by various academic scholars in the 1990s and was perhaps best refined by the Shadow Financial Regulatory Committee in *Reforming Bank Capital.*

38. We would apply the subordinated debt requirement only to the large banks that are subject to the Basel Accord and that are capable of selling these securities to investors on a routine basis. Some, or perhaps many, large banks may not be happy about having to live with a subordinated debt mandate. But they should be mollified

to some extent by the fact that the interest on such debt is fully tax deductible in all Basel countries (unlike dividends, which are not deductible).

39. See Hufbauer et al. (forthcoming).

40. Tariff data are from Burtless (1998).

41. For example, in the United States, the Coalition of Service Industries, the Investment Company Institute, and the Securities Industry Association, among others, all urged the U.S. special trade representative to assure market access for a wide range of service industries in various free trade agreements (FTAs) and in the WTO.

42. For example, in connection with the negotiation of the Australia–U.S. FTA, the U.S.-based Coalition for Service Industries expressed concern to the U.S. special trade representative about Australia's system of screening foreign firms for entry into that country's market.

Chapter 3. Finance and the "War on Terror"

1. Their statements are cited in Wechsler (2001). For another account, see Cohen (2001).

2. See Reuter and Truman (2004:1). In our view, this volume provides the most in-depth analysis of anti–money laundering efforts in the U.S. and other countries to date.

3. Statistics cited in Reuter and Truman (2004) and Wechsler (2001).

4. The formal name of this body is the Organized Crime Drug Enforcement Task Force. Also included on the task force, in addition to Justice, are the Treasury and Transportation departments.

5. Reuter and Truman (2004) report 164 offenses—covering virtually all serious crimes—that are now "predicate" acts to anti–money laundering laws. The authors note, however, that until the Patriot Act of 2001, foreign corruption was not a predicate crime for a money laundering offense in the United States. Other violations that may be committed abroad still are not covered as predicate offenses.

6. The "know your customer" regime has turned out to be as important, if not more important, in preventing identity theft—largely domestic activity—as it has in addressing money laundering. In July 2004, President Bush signed the Identity Theft Penalty Enhancement Act, which adds two years to the prison sentences of people who use stolen credit card numbers and other personal data in the commission of a crime. Individuals who use this information to commit a terrorist act would get an extra five years at sentencing.

7. See Levine (2004:31). Even the inspector general of the Department of Homeland Security reported in late 2004 that a megalist had not then been compiled. See Block and Fields (2004:1).

8. This is consistent with the conclusions of various studies of sanctions, which document that many countries must enforce them if they are to have any chance of success. See, e.g., Haass and O'Sullivan (2000), Elliot et al. (forthcoming), and Collins and Bowdoin (1999).

9. These countries are the Cook Islands, Indonesia, Nigeria, and the Philippines.

10. See Financial Action Task Force (2003).

11. See Pillar (1993:93).

12. See ibid. (1993:96).

13. See Department of the Treasury (2003). The six state sponsors of terrorism that the Treasury had identified as of this report included Cuba, Iran, Iraq, Libya, North Korea, and Syria.

14. See National Commission on Terrorist Attacks (2004:57).

15. There are other international efforts in place to counter money laundering in particular, including financial supervision through the Basel Committee; the International Organization of Securities Commissions (IOSCO); and International Association of Insurance Supervisors (IAIS); regional anti–money laundering task forces in Europe and the Organization of American States; and institutions engaged in legal and criminal enforcement matters, notably the Egmont Group of Financial Intelligence Units and Interpol.

16. See Greenberg et al. (2002:14).

17. See Hovanesian and Fairlamb (2003:102).

18. See FINCEN (2000:2). More recent data are from Reuter and Truman (2004).

19. This was dramatically illustrated during the summer of 2004, when it was revealed that Riggs National Bank, whose main office is located right across the street from the Treasury Department, was being investigated for being too lax in its compliance with AML rules.

20. See United States General Accounting Office (2003).

21. See Greenberg et al. (2002).

22. See Pillar (1993:94).

23. See Eisenberg and Burger (2004:40).

24. UN Report (summarized in FT.com, August 31, 2004).

25. Quoted in Duffy and Waller (2003:31).

26. See National Commission on Terrorist Attacks (2004:382–83). The commission predicts that financial regulation will be more a means of intelligence gathering than of cutting off the terrorists' lifeline. See also Weiss (2004).

27. See Reuter and Truman (2004:93–103).

28. Ibid. The estimate is that "2–3% of total US government regulatory and enforcement expenditures might be attributable to the AML regime." While government estimates are closer to 2 percent, they do not include expenditures by the Federal Reserve. When this is adjusted for, 3 percent appears more reasonable. The state and local estimates are based on "ready reckoning": total state and local consumption expenditures are approximately 1.7 times those at the federal level, but most AML enforcement and prevention is a federal responsibility. Taking these two factors into account, Reuter and Truman double the federal expenditure to arrive at total government costs.

29. See KPMG International (2004:9).

30. See Little-Gill (2003). Amounts include legal fees to create CIP, systems and document costs, information collection and verification costs, resolution of discrepancies, and record retention. Additional annual costs include costs to provide oversight on intermediary CIPs associated with wholesaler agreements, reimbursement for Intermediary CIP/AML management programs, annual training programs and compliance oversight, and additional auditing fee expenses.

31. See Reuter and Truman (2004:98–99). These estimates are drawn from studies for banks by the accounting firm Grant Thornton in 1992 and 1993. Reuter and Truman take the $240 million and $600 million estimated as the cost to banks in those years, scale it by nominal GDP growth to produce a figure of $1 billion in 2003, and then raise it to $1.5 billion to account for the increase in regulation. They double the banking figure to arrive at a total for the entire industry of $3 billion. They then cross-check this estimate with studies on the UK AML regime by KPMG and Pricewaterhouse Coopers in 2003.

32. See Reuter and Truman (2004:101–02). Reuter and Truman base this on the fact that financial institutions are able to shift up to a third of their gross financial costs to the consumer. While these costs would be factored into the previous figure of $3 billion, they add an additional $1 billion on top of that as additional "costs to the general public." They admit, however, that they have "no empirical basis" for these estimates.

33. See Simpson (2004:1).

34. See Krueger and Laitin (2004:8–13).

35. For a sample of such cases, see FINCEN (2000:16–23). Many of these cases involve variations of fraud and are unrelated to drug trafficking or money laundering.

36. Interview with Stephen Flynn, January 21, 2005. Figure assumes 18 million containers moved five times a year.

37. See Flynn (2004:17–35).

38. Interview with Stephen Flynn, January 21, 2005.

39. See Pillar (1993:94).

40. See Office of National Drug Control Policy (2004).

Chapter 4. Capital Markets Sanctions

Epigraph: Quoted in Alden (2000).

1. We owe these metaphors to the late Joseph Campbell (Campbell and Moyers, 1991).

2. See Swindell (2002).

3. The official name of the committee was the "Select Committee on U.S. National Security and Military/Commercial Concerns with the People's Republic of China."

4. PRC = People's Republic of China, PLA = People's Liberation Army

5. See Hiltzik and Romney (1999).

6. See Mulvenon (1997). See also Johnson (1999:44–51).

7. See May (1999:11).

8. The full name of the commission was the "Commission to Assess the Organization of the Federal Government to Combat the Proliferation of Weapons of Mass Destruction."

9. See Pener (2001).

10. "It's hard to say what exactly was the cause, but we're just grateful that it happened and we're hopeful it would be permanent," according to a D'Amato aide. See Karey (1997).

11. See Corzine and Thornhill (1997).

12. See Luce (1997).

13. See BBC (1997).

14. Ibid.

15. See, for example, *Euroweek* (1997).

16. The claim in Pener (2001) is backed by a footnote referring to another Casey Institute publication that says nothing whatsoever about Gazprom's debt issue.

17. See Pavey (1997).

18. Ibid.

19. See Corzine and Thornhill (1997).

20. See Agence France Presse (1997).

21. See Balz (1998).

22. See *Oil and Gas Journal* (1998).

23. See Interfax News Agency (2004).

24. See Diamond (2003).

25. See Lin (2000).

26. Ibid. (1999).

27. "The AFL-CIO led a patchwork alliance of labor unions, Republican lawmakers and Tibetan monks who accused the company of human-rights abuses and planning sweeping layoffs in China. But in Hong Kong, where the protests were a sideshow, analysts said PetroChina was handicapped by the market's indifference to companies that deliver their products through steel pipes rather than digital ones. 'Investors are focusing on high-tech dreams,' said Andrew Look, a director at Prudential Portfolio Managers (Asia) Ltd. 'This is an old-economy animal. For investors looking for action, they are going to look elsewhere' " (Landler, 2000).

28. See Pener (2001:47).

29. See *Petroleum Intelligence Weekly* (2004).

30. "Warren Buffett" includes the companies he controls, as per PetroChina's December 31, 2003 annual report filed with the SEC.

31. See Pener (2001:88).

32. See Vick (2001).

33. See *Calgary Herald* (2001).

34. See, for example, Cattaneo (2002).

35. From his testimony before the Senate Banking, Housing and Urban Affairs Committee, Subcommittee on Financial Institutions and Regulatory Relief (see Solomon, 1997).

36. See William J. Casey Institute of the Center for Security Policy (2001).

37. See Martin (2001).

38. See Alden (2001).

39. US economic sanctions are administered by the Treasury's Office of Foreign Assets Control (see http://www.treas.gov/ofac/).

40. See Unger (2002).

41. See Alden (2001).

42. See Donaldson (2004).

43. See Burns (2004).

44. See Zagaris (2004).

45. See Gaffney (2001).

46. See Repetto et al. (2002:30)

47. Ibid. (2002:iv).

48. Ibid. (2002:24).

49. See Hansard (2004).

50. See Diamond (2003).

51. See, for example, Pener (2001:1,3).

52. Item 101 of SEC Regulation S-K. Emphasis added.

53. See Robinson, Jr. (1999).

54. See Chernoff (2004).

55. See Mulvenon (1997).

56. See Robinson, Jr. (1999).

57. When weighted by market cap, the ratio declines to 3:1 for European firms but rises to 6:1 for mainland Chinese firms.

58. See Pener (2001:21).

59. See Senate Banking, Housing and Urban Affairs Committee (2000).

60. See Thompson (2000).

61. See Pener (2001:85).

62. See, for example, Diamond (2003).

Chapter 5. The Security Dimensions of Currency Crises

Epigraph: February 23, 1998, quoted in Snyder, Scott, and Richard H. Solomon, "Beyond the Asian Financial Crisis: Challenges and Opportunities for U.S. Leadership," Special Report 29, United States Institute of Peace, April 1998.

1. There were clearly threats to U.S. banking stability, however, most notably from the 1998 collapse of Long-Term Capital Management, which had borrowed enormous sums from large US banks

2. "Today, an economic crisis anywhere can affect economies everywhere. Recent months have brought serious financial problems to Thailand, Indonesia, South Korea and

beyond. Why should Americans be concerned about this? . . . they are our strategic partners. Their stability bolsters our security" (January 27, 1998). And from an interview with former Clinton Council of Economic Advisors Chair Laura D'Andrea Tyson: "You're, on balance, much better off having healthy trading partners than you are having debilitated trading partners. You're much better off if you can spend a couple billion dollars to prevent a debt default in South Korea than if South Korea defaults and you end up having to pick up the bill for work that South Korea was going to do with North Korea for a nuclear reactor. So you have to realize, and I think the president instinctively realizes this, that in the global system in which we now live, we can't distinguish very clearly between our military security, our national security, and our economic security. They're all part of the same system." http://globetrotter.berkeley.edu/conversations/Tyson/tyson-con7. html

3. Some would claim that this *was* a feature of the U.S. stock market, in the form of a so-called Greenspan put. This was the notion that the Federal Reserve was propping up the stock market at unrealistic levels through an implicit promise to cut interest rates should the market take a dive.

4. See *The Economist* (2004).

5. See Atinc and Walton (1998).

6. http://www.stratwar.com/Countries_Indonesia_Bali_President.htm

7. See, for example, Jawar Hassan (1999).

8. See Sanger (1997).

9. The previous limits were 7 percent for foreign individuals and 26 percent combined foreign ownership. See Reuters (1999).

10. See *Korea Times* (1998).

11. Ibid.

12. Testimony before the House International Relations Committee, Asia and Pacific Subcommittee. See Roth (1998).

13. "The United States Security Strategy for the Asia-Pacific Region," available online at: http://usinfo.state.gov/regional/ea/easec/easr98.htm

14. See Blank (1999:19).

15. Source of defense expenditure statistics: Stockholm International Peace Research Institute (SIPRI).

16. See Simon (1998).

17. See, for example, Cossa (1998).

18. See, for example, Buszynski (1999).

19. Ibid.

20. For example, the Philippines signed a Visiting Forces Agreement with the United States in February 1998, allowing joint training sessions between the United States and Filipino navies, and agreed to joint naval exercises with South Korea, Malaysia, and Vietnam (ibid.).

21. See, for example, CSCAP, (1999); Brandon (2000); and Progressive Policy Institute (2004).

22. See, for example, Bulkeley (2003); Dillon (2000); Chalk (2002); Smead (2001).

23. See Kontogeorgopoulos (1999).

24. See BBC News (1998).

25. See Buszynski (1999).

26. See, for example, Flanagan, Frost, and Kugler (2001)

27. See Frost, Rann, and Chin (2003).

28. See, for example, Laksamana.net (2002).

29. See, for example, Scott Tyson (2002); and Clamor (2002).

30. See, for example, the statement of Australian Labor Party foreign affairs spokesman Kevin Rudd in Kerin (2003).

31. See Scott Tyson (2002).

32. See Global Organized Crime Project of the Center for Strategic and International Studies (2000).

33. Senate Armed Services testimony (March 23, 1999:2), available online at: http://armed-services.senate.gov/statemnt/1999/990323rl.pdf

34. Senate Armed Services testimony (March 23, 1999:9, 11), available online at: http://armed-services.senate.gov/statemnt/1999/990323ew.pdf

35. See Bunn (1998).

36. See Dalton (1999).

37. See Hoffman (1998).

38. See Nuclear Threat Initiative (2003).

39. See Williams (1999).

40. See Stratfor (2003).

41. See Faiola (2002).

42. Ibid.

43. See Rohter (2003).

44. See Organization of American States (2002).

45. See United Nations Development Program (2004).

46. See Bureau for International Narcotics and Law Enforcement Affairs (1996).

47. See Federal Research Division of the Library of Congress (2003).

48. See *O Estado de São Paulo* (2003).

49. See Meirelles Passos (2001).

50. See Wishart (2002).

51. Interview with Defense Intelligience Agency Argentina Desk Officer (ibid.).

52. See Trinkunas and Boureston, (2002).

53. See Hill (2003:3–4).

Chapter 6. The Economics of Financial Crises

1. See Roubini and Setser (2004). Quote is from an earlier 2003 working-paper version, page 18.

2. See Reinhart, Rogoff, and Savastano (2003a).

3. See Goldstein and Turner (2004)

4. Ibid.

5. Ibid.

6. See Gray (1999).

7. See Worrell and Leon (2001).

8. This argument is made by the intellectual founders of the "Original Sin" school, which focuses on the systematic inability of most developing countries to sell their debt abroad in domestic currency. See, for example, Eichengreen, Hausmann, and Panizza (2003).

9. Eichengreen, Hausmann, and Panizza (2003) recommend that IFIs and G-10 governments commit to issuing debt in a new emerging-market currency basket index, which is supposed to create liquidity that will allow developing countries to issue debt in such an index, rather than in dollars. The problem would remain that the public as well as private sectors in developing countries are still likely to conclude that financing costs will be vastly lower for dollar debt. If so, global welfare is likely to be higher if governments simply stop manufacturing currencies that locals as well as foreigners do not want. Throughout all the countries hit by the Asia crisis, residents and domestic institutions were themselves choosing to borrow in dollars rather than local currency. And whereas macroeconomists have a tendency reflexively to condemn private dollar borrowing as risky behavior, domestic-currency debt is also risky where, as in Asia, governments openly pledge their willingness to defend the exchange rate with high real interest rates. See, for example, Jeanne (2002).

10. See IMF (2003).

11. See Allen and Gale (2002).

12. This is the case unless the exchange rate is only being "managed" for the purposes of achieving the inflation target.

13. See Fatás and Mihov (2003).

14. See Obstfeld and Taylor (1998).

15. 3.7 percent versus 2.3 percent. See ibid.

16. See Hausmann (1999).

17. See Mill (1894:176).

18. See Bordo (1999).

19. Ibid. (1999:10).

20. See Eichengreen and Hausmann (1999). The fact that such a small number of currencies has come to dominate international markets has been widely attributed to network externalities in cross-border transactions (see, for example, Kiyotaki, Matsuyama, and Matsui, 1992). History can play a large part in creating such externalities: witness the disproportionately prominent role of the pound sterling in international transactions.

21. Gallego and Hernandez (2003) also show that a major component of Chile's capital controls regimes, a non-interest-bearing deposit requirement on foreign borrowing, increased the cost of borrowing to Chilean firms.

22. See Eichengreen, Hausmann, and Panizza (2003).

23. This finding holds after correcting for other variables that explain trade across provinces or states. See Berg and Borensztein (2003:83).

24. See the meta-analysis of Rose (2002).

25. See Frankel and Rose (2000).

26. This would define regions within which labor and capital were maximally mobile and across which macroeconomic shocks would be maximally asymmetric.

27. This assumption is known as "sticky prices," or, in the specific case of wages, the notion that workers suffer from "money illusion" in failing to recognize and react to the impact of inflation on their living standards.

28. See Dornbusch (2000).

29. See Calvo and Reinhart (2000a).

30. See Calvo and Reinhart (2000b:2).

31. See the analysis and literature survey in Panizza, Stein, and Talvi (2003).

32. See Calvo and Reinhart (2000a).

33. See Dornbusch, Litan, and Mussa (1999).

34. See Hayek (1976) on justice.

35. See Mundell (2003:34).

36. Edwards and Magendzo (2002) find a mean inflation difference of 55 percentage points in favor of dollarizers. Excluding nondollarizers with experiences of hyperinflation still leaves dollarizers a 3.5 to 5.7 percentage point advantage, depending on the composition of the control group. Using medians, the difference is 5.2 percentage points, or 1.92 to 4.45 percentage points using control groups excluding those experiencing hyperinflation.

37. See, for example, Eichengreen, Hausmann, and Panizza (2003) and Goldstein and Turner (2004).

38. Von Furstenberg (2003) points out that holding such long-term investments in local currency provides less real-value assurance than denominating in major internationally traded currencies.

39. See Dornbusch (2000).

40. See the Senate Banking Committee testimony of Michael Gavin (Gavin, 1999).

41. See Hinds (2003).

42. See Burger and Warnock (2002).

43. See Reinhart, Rogoff, and Savastano (2003b) and De Nicolo, Honohan, and Ize (2003).

44. See von Furstenberg (2003).

45. See Antinolfi and Keister (2001); Chang and Velasco (2000); Mishkin (1999); and Fischer (1999).

46. See Hinds (2003), who provides numerous recent examples of massive central bank dollar borrowing during crises around the world.

47. See Munter and Paivi (2004).

48. See Salvatore (2003).

49. See Leblang (1997).

50. See Salvatore (2003).

51. See Drazen (2002).

52. See Burger and Warnock (2002); Reinhart, Rogoff, and Savastano (2003b); Khan, Senhadji and Smith (2001); and Caprio and Honohan (2001).

53. Reinhart, Rogoff, and Savastano (2003b) found this to be the case in 98 percent of the 85 de facto dollarized countries they studies.

54. See Corden (2002) and Martinez and Werner (2001).

55. See Moreno-Villalaz (1999).

56. See Milverton (2000).

Chapter 7. Global Capital Flows and U.S. Foreign Policy

1. See Roubini and Setser (2004).

2. See Rubin (2003:5).

3. This concern at the top of the State Department was cited by Robert Rubin (2003:230–32).

4. Quoted in Blustein (2001:139).

5. See ibid. (2001:138).

6. See Rubin and Weisberg (2003:232–33).

7. See ibid. (2003:277–79).

8. Quotes from Blustein (2001: 228–29).

9. Quote ibid. (2001:230).

10. See Rubin and Weisberg (2003:258).

11. See Hill (2004).

12. Interview, May 4, 2004.

13. See Rubin and Weisberg (2003:239).

14. See ibid. (2003:278).

15. See Blustein (2003), quoting from the *Wall Street Journal Europe*. Blustein also cites a Merrill Lynch client report saying that GKOs posed "little risk of devaluation with the new IMF loans," and that "the IMF loan virtually assures a stable exchange rate, at least through the summer."

16. See Rubin and Weisberg (2003:263).

17. See Piga (2001) and Steil (2001).

18. See Galvis (2003).

19. See, for example, White (2002).

20. See Roubini and Setser (2004).

21. See Wolf (2004).

22. See Roubini and Setser (2004).

23. See Summers (1992:32)

24. See Truman (2000).

25. Alternatively, the United States could provide the dollarizing central bank with a one-time allotment of newly issued dollars to replace its reserves, which will in turn be used to provide the initial circulating stock of dollars in the country. In

exchange, the United States would receive a fixed amount of the non-interest-bearing domestic currency to be retired, which would be held as collateral. In the case of Argentina, this would be equivalent to about $16 billion. If the dollarizing country should de-dollarize in the future, the currency swap would be reversed at the same exchange rate. In this manner, dollarizers would avoid any seigniorage loss. Moreover, the United States would still receive a substantial seigniorage windfall as economic growth in the dollarized country increased demand for non-interest-bearing dollars. (See Barro, 1999.) The obvious risk in this arrangement is that a de-dollarizing government would fail to honor its swap commitment and choose to introduce new notes instead, invalidating the old ones held by the Fed. Such behavior would be sufficiently hostile as to indicate relations ruptured by matters sufficiently more grave than a squabble over this stock of cash.

26. Such standards include those described in the Core Principles for Effective Banking Supervision established by the Basel Committee on Banking Supervision of the Bank for International Settlements.

27. See Kolbe (2004).

28. See Altig (2002).

29. For 1984–2003, end-of-year (December) data were used for the foreign official holdings of U.S. Treasuries as well as total U.S. Treasuries outstanding. Data for 2004 are the latest available from the U.S. Treasury Department, i.e., September (total U.S. Treasuries) and November (foreign official holdings). For 1984–2003, annual data were used for the current account balance. The estimate for 2004 is based on the latest available data from the Bureau of Economic Analysis. The estimate is the sum of current account balance over the four consecutive quarters ending third quarter 2004.

30. See M. Murenbeeld & Associates, Inc. (2002).

31. See, for example, Giles and Johnson (2004); Andrews (2004); and Brooke and Bradsher (2004).

32. See, for example, Chinn (2004).

33. See, for example, Rubin, Orszag, and Sinai (2004).

34. ASEAN is comprised of Brunei, Cambodia, Indonesia, Laos, Malaysia, Myanmar, the Philippines, Singapore, Thailand, and Vietnam.

35. See Courchene and Harris (2003).

36. See ECOFIN (2000).

37. See European Commission (2000).

38. See Bratkowski and Rostowski (2001).

39. See, for example, Sulling (2002).

Chapter 8. The Future of Financial Statecraft

1. A book-length study of IMF lending concluded that "where US foreign policy interests come more heavily into play, such as in Russia, . . . the IMF cannot credibly commit to enforcing the loans-for-policy contract " (Stone, 2002). This finding

was recently backed by a former top IMF official, who stated that "while the G7 helped to create an important role for the IMF in Russia, its political and bilateral interests at the same time caused a weakening of the IMF's influence," and that the United States "effectively determined the collective position" of the G-7 (John Odling-Smee, quoted in the *Financial Times,* see Jack, 2004.)

2. See Wolf (2004:320).

REFERENCES

Agence France Presse. "Gazprom to Invest Over $600 Million in Iran Gas Project." November 25, 1997.

Alden, Edward. "US Legislators Want Markets to Sway Sudan." *Financial Times,* November 2, 2000.

———. "SEC Chief Inherits Disclosure Bombshell." *Financial Times,* May 11, 2001.

Allen, Franklin, and Douglas Gale. "Liquidity, Asset Prices and Systemic Risk." In *Proceedings of the 3rd Central Bank Conference on Risk Measurement and Systemic Risk,* Bank for International Settlements, 2002.

Altig, David E. "Why Is Stable Money Such a Big Deal?" May 1, Federal Reserve Bank of Cleveland. Available at: http://www.clevelandfed.org/research/ Com2002/ 0501.pdf, 2002.

Andrews, Edmund L. "Foreign Interest Appears to Flag as Dollar Falls." *New York Times,* November 27, 2004.

Antinolfi, Gaetano, and Todd Keister. "Dollarization as a Monetary Arrangement for Emerging Market Economies." In *Federal Reserve Bank of St. Louis Review,* November/December, Federal Reserve Bank of St. Louis, 2001.

Atinc, Tamar Manuelyan, and Michael Walton. "Social Consequences of the East Asian Financial Crisis." World Bank, Available at: http://www. worldbank.org/eapsocial/library/socconsq/eacrisis2.pdf, 1998.

Baldwin, David Allen. *Economic Statecraft.* Princeton: Princeton University Press, 1985.

Balz, Dan. "U.S. Eases Stand on Cuba, Iran Sanctions; Helms Condemns, Europe Hails Move." *Washington Post,* May 19, 1998.

Barro, Robert. "Let the Dollar Reign from Seattle to Santiago." *Wall Street Journal,* March 8, 1999.

Baumol, William. "The Red Queen Game." Unpublished manuscript, 2003.

BBC. "Gas Company Cancels Credit Accord with US Bank." *BBC Summary of World Broadcasts,* December 22, 1997.

BBC News. "Indonesia: Why Ethnic Chinese are Afraid." February 12, BBC News, 1998.

Benston, George, and George Kauffman. "Regulating Financial Services." In William S. Haraf and Rose Marie Kushmeider, eds., *Restructuring Banking and Financial Services in America.* American Enterprise Institute, 1988.

Berg, Andrew, and Eduardo R. Borensztein. "The Pros and Cons of Full Dollarization." In Dominick Salvatore, James W. Dean, and Thomas D. Willett, eds., *The Dollarization Debate,* pp. 72–101. New York: Oxford University Press, 2003.

Blank, Stephen J. "East Asia in Crisis: The Security Implications of the Collapse of Economic Institutions." February 5, Strategic Studies Institute monograph, 1999.

Blustein, Paul. *The Chastening: Inside the Crisis That Rocked the Global Financial System and Humbled the IMF.* PublicAffairs, 2003.

Bordo, Michael D. *The Gold Standard and Related Regimes: Collected Essays.* New York: Cambridge University Press, 1999.

Brandon, John J. "High-Seas Piracy is Booming. It's Time to Fight Harder." *Christian Science Monitor,* December 27, 2000.

Bratkowski, Andrzej, and Jacek Rostowski. "The EU Attitude to Unilateral Euroization: Misunderstandings, Real Concerns and Ill-Designed Admission Criteria." January, CASE Institute Working Paper, Warsaw and Central European University, 2001.

Brooke, James, and Keith Bradsher. "Dollar's Fall Tests Nerve of Asia's Central Bankers." *New York Times,* December 4, 2004.

Bulkeley, Jennifer C. "Regional Cooperation on Maritime Piracy: A Prelude to Greater Multilateralism in Asia." *Journal of Public and International Affairs* 14 (Spring 2003).

Bunn, Matthew. "Loose Nukes Fears: Anecdotes of the Current Crisis." *PBS Frontline,* December 5. Available at: http://www.pbs.org/wgbh/pages/ frontline/ shows/russia/readings/fears.html, 1998.

Bureau for International Narcotics and Law Enforcement Affairs. *International Narcotics Control Strategy Report.* March, U.S. Department of State. Available at: http://www.hri.org/docs/USSD-INCSR/95/Financial/ Chapter11.html, 1996.

Burger, John D., and Francis E. Warnock. "Diversification, Original Sin, and International Bond Portfolios." Board of Governors of the Federal Reserve System, 2002.

Burns, Arthur F. "The Need for Order in International Finance." Address before Columbia Graduate School of Business. Available at: http://www.rich.frb. org/pubs/economic_review/pdfs/er630403.pdf, 1977.

Burns, Judith. "SEC to Review Corporate Ties with Rogue States." February 9, Associated Press, 2004.

Burtless, Gary, Robert Z. Lawrence, Progressive Policy Institute, Twentieth Century Fund. *Globaphobia: Confronting Fears About Open Trade*. Washington: Brookings Institution Press, 1998.

Buszynski, Leszek. "The Impact of the Asian Financial Crisis on Southeast Asia." IUJ Research Institute Working Paper, Asia Pacific Series 14, 1999.

Calgary Herald, "Talisman Will Be Missed: Calgary Company Exercised Moderating Influence on Sudan Regime." *Calgary Herald*, June 30, 2001.

Calvo, Guillermo A., and Carmen M. Reinhart. "Fear of Floating." NBER Working Paper No. 7993, 2000a.

———. "Reflections on Dollarization." In Alberto Alesina and Robert J. Barro, eds., *Currency Unions*, June 16, pp. 39–48. Stanford: Hoover Institution Press, 2000b.

Campbell, Joseph, and Bill Moyers. *The Power of Myth*. New York: Anchor, 1991.

Caprio, Gerard, and Patrick Honohan. *Finance for Growth: Policy Choices in a Volatile World*. World Bank and New York: Oxford University Press, 2001.

Cattaneo, Claudia. "Talisman Raises £250M: Denies It Went to Europe to Avoid Sudan Controversy." *Financial Post*, April 6, 2002.

Chalk, Peter. "Threats to the Maritime Environment: Piracy and Terrorism." SeaCurity conference presentation, Ispra, Italy, October 28–30, 2002.

Chang, Roberto, and Velasco, Andres. "Financial Fragility and the Exchange Rate Regime." *Journal of Economic Theory* 92 (2000): 1–34.

Chernoff, Joel. "Report's Aftermath: Public Plans at Odds over a 'Messy' Issue; Some Want to Investigate if Stocks They Own Have Ties to Terrorism." *Pensions and Investments*, April 5, 2004.

Chinn, Menzie D. "Incomes, Exchange Rates and the US Trade Deficit, Once Again." *International Finance* 7:3 (2004).

Clamor, Concepcion B. "Terrorism and Southeast Asia: A Philippine Perspective." May, Asia-Pacific Area Network. Available at: http://www.apan-info.net/partners/uploads/Terrorism%20and%20Southeast%20Asia.pdf, 2002.

Clinton, William J. "State of the Union Address." January 27, 1998.

Cohen, Adam. "Banking on Secrecy." *Time*, October 22, 2001.

Cohen, Benjamin J. *Banks and the Balance of Payments: Private Lending in the International Adjustment Process*. Lanham, Md.: Rowman and Littlefield, 1981.

———. *In Whose Interest?* Council on Foreign Relations and New Haven: Yale University Press, 1986.

———, ed. *American Foreign Economic Policy: Essays and Comments*. New York: Harper and Row, 1968.

Collins, Joseph J., and Gabrielle D. Bowdoin. *Beyond Unilateral Economic Sanctions: Better Alternatives for U.S. Foreign Policy*. Center for Strategic and International Studies, 1999.

Cooper, Richard N., and Jane Little. "Competition and Opportunity." *Federal Reserve Bank of Boston Regional Review,* Third Quarter, pp. 16–23, 2001.

Corden, W. Max. *Too Sensational: On the Choice of Exchange Rate Regimes.* Cambridge: MIT Press, 2002.

Corzine, Robert, and John Thornhill. "Gazprom to Add $3bn Borrowing to Bridge Loan." *Financial Times,* November 4, 1997.

Cossa, Ralph A. "Security Implications of Conflict in the South China Sea: Exploring Potential Triggers of Conflict." *Pacific Forum CSIS Special Report,* March, Pacific Forum CSIS, 1998.

Courchene, Thomas J., and Richard G. Harris. "North American Currency Integration: A Canadian Perspective." In Dominick Salvatore, James W. Dean, and Thomas D. Willett, eds., *The Dollarization Debate.* New York: Oxford University Press, 2003.

Cronin, Richard P. "Asian Financial Crisis: An Analysis of U.S. Foreign Policy Interests and Options." January 28, CRS Report for Congress, 1999.

CSCAP. "Report of the 5th Meeting of the Council for Security Cooperation in the Asia Pacific Working Group on Transnational Crime." May 23–25, Council for Security Cooperation in the Asia Pacific, 1999.

Dalton, Toby. "U.S. Programs Face Growing Russian Threat." *Proliferation Brief* 2, no. 4 (March 4). Carnegie Endowment for International Peace, 1999.

De Nicolo, Gianni, Patrick Honohan, and Alain Ize. "Dollarization of the Banking System: Good or Bad?" World Bank Policy Research Working Paper 3116, 2003.

Department of the Treasury. "Terrorist Assets Report, Calendar Year 2002." U.S. Department of the Treasury, 2003.

Diamond, Stephen F. "The PetroChina Syndrome: Regulating Capital Markets in the Anti-Globalization Era." Cornell Law School Working Papers Series, 2003.

Dillon, Dana R. "Piracy in Asia: A Growing Barrier to Maritime Trade." June 22, Heritage Foundation, Backgrounder #1379, 2000.

Dinc, Serdar, and Patrick McGuire. "Did Investors Regard Real Estate as 'Safe' during the 'Japanese Bubble' in the 1980s?" Paper presented at a conference on the Japanese economy in Tokyo jointly organized by the NBER, CEPR, CIRJE, and EIJS, September 19–20, 2003.

Donaldson, William H. "Statement of William H. Donaldson, Chairman, U.S. Securities and Exchange Commission before the Subcommittee on Commerce, Justice, State and the Judiciary Committee on House Appropriations." March 31, Federal Document Clearing House Congressional Testimony, 2004.

Dornbusch, Rudiger. "Fewer Monies, Better Monies." Available at: http://web.mit.edu/rudi/www/media/PDFs/FewerMonies.pdf, 2000.

Dornbusch, Rudiger, Robert Litan, and Michael Mussa. "Panel on the Future for International Financial Institutions." In Susan M. Collins and Robert Z.

Lawrence, eds., *Brookings Trade Forum, 1999*. Washington: Brookings Institution, 1999.

Drazen, Allen. "Central Bank Independence, Democracy, and Dollarization." *Journal of Applied Economics* 5, no. 1 (2002): 1–17.

Duffy, Michael, and Douglas Waller. "Is Rumsfeld Losing His Mojo?; Facing Persistent Enemy Attacks in Iraq, the Defense Secretary Now Finds Himself Fighting Battles at Home Too." *Time Magazine*, November 3, 2003.

ECOFIN. "Exchange-Rate Strategies for Accession Countries—Council Conclusions." November 7, ECOFIN, Press Release 12925/00, 2000.

Economist, The. "A Remedy for Financial Turbulence?" *The Economist*, April 17, 2004.

Edwards, Sebastian, and I. Igal Magendzo. "Dollarization and Economic Performance: What Do We Really Know?" *International Journal of Finance and Economics* 8 (2003): 351–63.

Eichengreen, Barry. "Capital Account Liberalization: What Do the Cross-Country Studies Tell Us?" Available at: http://emlab.berkeley.edu/users/eichengr/research/bourgignonpaper6.pdf, 2001.

Eichengreen, Barry, and Ricardo Hausmann. "Exchange Rates and Financial Fragility." NBER Working Paper 7418. Available at: http://papers.nber.org/papers/w7418, 1999.

Eichengreen, Barry, Ricardo Hausmann, and Ugo Panizza. "Original Sin: The Pain, the Mystery, and the Road to Redemption." Prepared for Currency and Maturity Mismatching conference, Inter-American Development Bank, November 21–22, 2002.

———. "The Pain of Original Sin." Available at: http://emlab.berkeley.edu/users/eichengr/research.html, 2003.

Eisenberg, Daniel, and Timothy J. Burger. "What We Know Now; TIME's Guide to the New Revelations about How Sept. 11 Happened." *Time Magazine*, June 28, 2004.

Elliot, Kimberly Ann, Jeffrey J. Schott, Gary Clyde Hufbauer, and Barbara Oegg. *Economic Sanctions Reconsidered*, 3d ed. Institute for International Economics, Forthcoming.

Estrella, Arturo. "The Cyclical Behavior of Optimal Bank Capital." *Journal of Banking and Finance* 28, no. 6 (2004): 1469–98.

European Commission. "Exchange Rate Strategies for EU Candidate Countries (Note for the Economic and Financial Committee)." August 22, European Commission, ECFIN/521/2000-EN, 2000.

Euroweek. "Gazprom Clarifies Plans for $3 Bn Autumn Bond Financing Bonanza." *Euroweek*, August 8, 1997.

Faiola, Anthony. "Economic Crisis Spurs Anger." May 19, Washington Post Foreign Service, 2002.

Fatás, Antonio, and Ilian Mihov. "The Case for Restricting Fiscal Policy Discretion." CEPR Discussion Paper 3277, 2002.

Federal Research Division of the Library of Congress. "Nations Hospitable to Organized Crime and Terrorism." October, Library of Congress, 2003.

Financial Action Task Force on Money Laundering. "The Forty Recommendations." June 20. Available at: http://www.fatf-gafi.org/dataoecd/38/47/34030579.PDF, 2003.

FINCEN, "The SAR Activity Review: Trends, Tips & Issues." October 2000.

Fischer, Stanley. "On the Need for an International Lender of Last Resort." *Journal of Economic Perspectives* 13 (Fall 1999): 85–104.

Flanagan, Stephen J., Ellen J. Frost, and Richard L. Kugler. *Challenges of the Global Century: Report of the Project on Globalization and National Security.* June, National Defense University, 2001.

Flynn, Stephen. *America the Vulnerable: How Our Government Is Failing to Protect Us from Terrorism.* New York: HarperCollins, 2004.

Frankel, Jeffrey A., and Andrew K. Rose. "Estimating the Effects of Currency Unions on Trade and Output." NBER Working Paper no. 7857, 2000.

Frost, Frank, Ann Rann, and Andrew Chin. "Terrorism in Southeast Asia." April 11, Parliamentary Library, Parliament of Australia. Available at: http://www.aph. gov.au/library/intguide/FAD/sea.htm, 2003.

Furfine, Craig. "Bank Portfolio Allocation: The Impact of Capital Requirements, Regulatory Monitoring and Economic Conditions." *Journal of Financial Services Research* 20, no. 1 (1999): 33–56.

Furman, J., Stiglitz, J. E., 1998. "Economic Crises: Evidence and Insights from East Asia." *Brookings Papers on Economic Activity* (2), 1–135.

Gaffney, Frank Jr. "Market Transparency at Work." *Washington Times,* July 3, 2001.

Gallego, Francisco A., and F. Leonardo Hernández. "Microeconomic Effects of Capital Controls: The Chilean Experience During the 1990s." Central Bank of Chile Working Paper 203. Available at: http://www.bcentral.cl/esp/estpub/estudios/dtbc/pdf/dtbc203.pdf, 2003.

Galvis, Sergio. "Sovereign Debt Restructurings—The Market Knows Best." *International Finance* 6, no. 1 (2003).

Gavin, Michael. "Prepared Testimony of Dr. Michael Gavin." July 15, Senate Banking Committee. Available at: http://banking.senate.gov/99_07hrg/071599/gavin.htm, 1999.

Giles, Chris, and Steve Johnson. "Dollar Down as Moscow Trails Case for Euro." *Financial Times,* November 24, 2004.

Global Organized Crime Project of the Center for Strategic and International Studies. "Russian Organized Crime." Center for Strategic and International Studies, 2000.

Goldstein, Morris, and Philip Turner. *Controlling Currency Mismatches in Emerging Markets.* Washington: Institute for International Economics, 2004.

Grant, James. "Day of Reckoning? Foreign Borrowers May Have Trouble Repaying Their Debts." *Barron's,* January 7, 1980.

Gray, Dale. "Assessment of Corporate Sector Value and Vulnerability: Links to Exchange Rate Crises and Financial Crises." World Bank Technical Paper no. 455, 1999.

Greenberg, Maurice R., William F. Wechsler, Lee S. Wolosky, Council on Foreign Relations, and United States General Accounting Office. *Terrorist Financing: Independent Task Force.* Washington: Council on Foreign Relations Press, 2002.

Greider, William F. *Secrets of the Temple.* New York: Touchstone, 1987.

Haass, Richard N., and Meghan O'Sullivan, eds. *Honey and Vinegar: Incentives, Sanctions and Foreign Policy.* Washington: Brookings Institution Press, 2000.

Haass, Richard N., ed. *Economic Sanctions and American Diplomacy.* Washington: Brookings Institution Press, 1998.

Hall, Brian J. "How Has the Basle Accord Affected Bank Portfolios?" June, Harvard Institute of Economic Research Discussion Paper no. 1642, 1993.

Hansard, Sara. "Environmental-Risk Question Looms: Would Lawsuits Result from More Disclosure?" *Investment News,* April 26, 2004.

Hausmann, Ricardo. "Should There Be Five Currencies or One Hundred and Five?" *Foreign Policy* 116 (1999): 65–79.

Hausmann, Ricardo, Michael Gavin, Carmen Pages-Serra, and Ernesto Stein. "Financial Turmoil and the Choice of Exchange Rate Regime." IADB Working paper no. 400, 1999.

Hayek, F. A. *Law, Legislation and Liberty. Volume 2, The Mirage of Social Justice.* London: Routledge and Kegan Paul, 1976.

Hill, Charles. "Commissionism." *Wall Street Journal,* July 23, 2004.

Hill, James T. "Statement by General James T. Hill United States Army Commander, United States Southern Command." March 12, Federal Document Clearing House Congressional Testimony, 2003.

Hiltzik, Michael A., and Lee Romney. "Experts Dispute Report's Claim on China Fronts." *Los Angeles Times,* May 27, 1999.

Hinds, Manuel. "Globalization, Dollarization and Country Risks in Developing Countries: The Case of El Salvador." Mimeo, 2003.

Hoffman, David. "Russian Nuclear Security Called Lax: Easy Access to Fuel, Failure to Pay Wages Alarm U.S. Experts." *Washington Post,* November 27, 1998.

Hufbauer, Gary Clyde, Jeffrey J. Schott, and Kimberly Ann Elliott. *Economic Sanctions Reconsidered,* 2d ed. Institute for International Economics, 1990.

Interfax News Agency. "International Consortium Completes $2 Billion Complex at South Pars Field in Iran." *Interfax News Agency News Bulletin,* July 5, 2004.

International Monetary Fund. "Selected Issues in Emerging Markets Financial Systems." *Global Financial Stability Report,* International Monetary Fund, 2000.

Jack, Andrew. "G7 'Interfered in IMF Bid to Push through Russia Reform.'" *Financial Times,* October 4, 2004.

Jawar Hassan, Mohamed. "Post-Crisis Asian Views of the West: Mounting Apprehensions." *PacNet Newsletter,* no. 46 (November 24), Pacific Forum CSIS, 1999.

Jeanne, Olivier. "Why Do Emerging Economies Borrow in Foreign Currency?" Prepared for Currency and Maturity Matchmaking: Redeeming Debt from Original Sin conference, Inter-American Development Bank, November 21–22, 2002.

Johnson, Chalmers. "In Search of a New Cold War." *Bulletin of the Atomic Scientists* 55, no. 5 (September/October 1999): 44–51.

Joint Economic Committee Staff. "Basics of Dollarization." Available at: http://users.erols.com/kurrency/basicsup.htm, 2000.

Karey, Gerald. "D'Amato Jubilant over Gazprom's Bond Cancellation." *Platts Oilgram News,* November 12, 1997.

Kerin, John. "US Aims at Terror Schools." *Australian Weekender,* October 4, 2003.

Khan, Mohsin, Abdelhak Senhadji, and Bruce Smith. "Inflation and Financial Depth." IMF Working Paper no. 01/44, 2001.

Kiyotaki, Nobuhiro, Kiminori Matsuyama, and Akihiko Matsui. "Toward a Theory of International Currency." Hoover Institution, e-92-6, 1992.

Kolbe, Jim. "Hearing of the Foreign Operations, Export Financing and Related Programs Subcommittee of the House House Appropriations Committee." May 20, Federal News Service, 2004.

Kontogeorgopoulos, Nick. "The Human Face of the Asian Crisis." *The IPE of the Asian Crisis,* August 12, University of Puget Sound. Available at: http://www.ups.edu/ipe/asiacrisis/, 1999.

Korea Times. "Will Anti-Americanism Resurface?" *Korea Times,* November 20, 1998.

KPMG International. *Global Anti-Money Laundering Survey 2004: How Banks are Facing up to the Challenge.* KPMG International, 2004.

Kreisler, Harry. "Laura D'Andrea Tyson Interview." *Conversations with History,* January 14. Available at http://globetrotter.berkeley.edu/conversations/Tyson/tyson-con7.html, 1998.

Krueger, Alan B., and David D. Laitin. "'Misunderestimating' Terrorism." *Foreign Affairs* (September/October 2004): 8–13.

Laksamana.net. "Indonesia's Hybrid Al-Qaeda?" February 4, Laksamana.net. Available at: http://www.laksamana.net/vnews.cfm?ncat=19&news_id=1961, 2002.

Landler, Mark. "China's Oil Company Goes Public with Whimper." *New York Times,* April 8, 2000.

Lasswell, Harold D. *Politics: Who Gets What, When, How.* New York: Meridian Books, 1958.

Leblang, David. "Domestic and Systemic Determinants of Capital Controls." *International Studies Quarterly* 41 (1997): 435–54.

Levine, Samantha. "Spinning Terror's Rolodex." *U.S. News and World Report,* February 2, 2004.

Lin, Ho Swee. "Poor Investor Response Forces China to Delay Two Listings." *Financial Times,* April 1, 2000.

———. "Investors Tread Warily in China Oilfields." *Financial Times,* December 23, 1999.

Little-Gill, Gavin. "What Will USA Patriot Act CIP Requirements Cost Mutual Funds? Upwards of $13 per New Relationship." TowerGroup, 2003.

Luce, Edward. "Emerging Market Borrowers Move to Loans." *Financial Times,* November 17, 1997.

Lugar, Richard G. "Prepared Statement of Senator Richard G. Lugar before the Senate Armed Services Committee, Emerging Threats Subcommittee," March 23, Federal News Service, 1999.

M. Murenbeeld & Associates, Inc. "An Analysis of Central Bank Gold Sales and Its Impact on the Gold Mining Industry in Canada." May. Available at: http:// www.nrcan.gc.ca/mms/mmc/2002/rmf.pdf, 2002.

Martin, David B. H. "Memo to SEC Acting Chairman Laura Unger." May 8, 2001.

Martinez, Lorenza, and Alejandro Werner. "The Exchange Rate Regime and the Currency Composition of Corporate Debt: The Mexican Experience." Prepared for Inter-American Seminar on Economics conference, NBER, July 20–21, 2001.

May, M. M., ed. "The Cox Committee Report: An Assessment." December, Center for International Security and Cooperation, Stanford University, 1999.

Meirelles Passos, Jose. "The Shadow of Bin Laden in Latin America." *O Globo,* October 29, Rio de Janeiro, 2001.

Mill, John Stuart. *Principles of Political Economy.* Volume 2. London: Macmillan, 1894.

Milverton, Damian. "IMF Official Cites Benefits of Dollarization." *Wall Street Journal,* May 17, 2000.

Mishkin, Frederic S. "Lessons from the Asian Crisis." *Journal of International Money and Finance* 18 (1999): 709–23.

Moreno-Villalaz, Juan Luis. "Cost of Using the Dollar as Currency." Mimeo. Available at: http://www.sinfo.net/juanluismoreno, 1998.

Mulvenon, James. "Chinese Military Commerce and U.S. National Security." June, RAND Center for Asia-Pacific Policy Working Paper, 1997.

Mundell, Robert. "Currency Areas, Exchange Rate Systems, and International Monetary Reform." In Dominick Salvatore, James W. Dean, and Thomas Willett, eds., *The Dollarization Debate.* New York: Oxford University Press, 2003.

Munter, Paivi, and Stefan Wagstyl. "Central Bank Acts to Prevent Financial Crisis." *Financial Times,* December 1, 2004.

National Commission on Terrorist Attacks. *The 9/11 Commission Report: Final Report of the National Commission on Terrorist Attacks Upon the United States.* New York: W. W. Norton, 2004

Nuclear Threat Initiative. "The Threat: Anecdotes of Nuclear Insecurity." Nuclear Threat Initiative. Available at: http://www.nti.org/e_research/cnwm/threat/anecdote.asp?print=true, 2003.

O Estado de São Paulo. "Terrorist Khalid Sheikh Mohammed's Passage Through Brazil Reported." *O Estado de São Paulo,* March 9, 2003.

Obstfeld, Maurice, and Alan M. Taylor. "The Great Depression as a Watershed: International Capital Mobility over the Long Run." In Michael D. Bordo, Claudia Goldin, and Eugene N. White, eds., *The Defining Moment: The Great Depression and the American Economy in the Twentieth Century.* Chicago: University of Chicago Press, 1998.

Office of National Drug Control Policy. "National Drug Control Strategy: FY 2005 Budget Summary." March. Available at: http://www.whitehousedrugpolicy.gov/publications/policy/budgetsum04/index.html, 2004.

Oil and Gas Journal. "U.S. Waives Sanctions on South Pars Field." *Oil and Gas Journal,* May 25, 1998.

Organization of American States. "High Quality Economic Policy Vital to Handling Region's Crisis." June 10, Organization of American States. Available at: http:// www.oas.org/OASpage/press_releases/press_release.asp?sCodigo=E-113/02, 2002.

O'Sullivan, Meghan L. *Shrewd Sanctions: Statecraft and State Sponsors of Terrorism.* Washington: Brookings Institution Press, 2003.

Panizza, Ugo, Ernesto Stein, and Ernesto Talvi. "Measuring Costs and Benefits of Dollarization: An Application to Central American and Caribbean Countries." In Eduardo Levy Yeyati and Federico Sturzenegger, eds., *Dollarization: Debates and Policy Alternatives.* Cambridge: MIT Press, 2003.

Pastor, Robert A. *Congress and the Politics of U.S. Foreign Economic Policy, 1929–1976.* Berkeley: University of California Press, 1980.

Pavey, Nigel. "Gazprom's Stunning Loan Debut." *Euromoney,* May 1997.

Peek, Joe. "Japanese Banking Problems: Implications for Lending in the United States." *New England Economic Review* (January-February 1999).

Pener, Adam. "Capital Markets Transparency and Security: The Nexus Between U.S.-China Security Relations and America's Capital Markets." June 29, William J. Casey Institute of the Center for Security Policy, 2001.

Perry, George L. "Policy Alternatives for 1974." *Brookings Papers on Economic Activity* I (1975).

Petroleum Intelligence Weekly. "CNPC Is Chinese Oil Firm to Watch." *Petroleum Intelligence Weekly,* February 11, 2004.

Piga, Gustavo. "Derivatives and Public Debt Management." International Securities Market Association, 2001.

Pillar, Paul R. *Terrorism and U.S. Foreign Policy.* Washington: Brookings Institution Press, 1993.

Progressive Policy Institute. "Piracy Rates Are Rising." *PPI Trade Fact of the Week.* March 10, Progressive Policy Institute, 2004

Reinhart, Carmen M., Kenneth S. Rogoff, and Miguel A. Savastano. "Debt Intolerance." In William Brainard and George Perry, eds., *Brookings Papers on Economic Activity* 1 (2003): 1–74. Washington: Brookings Institution, 2003a.

———. "Addicted to Dollars." NBER Working Paper no. 10015, 2003b.

Repetto, Robert, Andrew MacSkimming, and Gustavo Carvajal Isunza. "Environmental Disclosure Requirements in the Securities Regulations and Financial Accounting Standards of Canada, Mexico and the United States." March 22, Commission for Environmental Cooperation, 2002.

Reuter, Peter, and Edwin M. Truman. *Chasing Dirty Money: Progress on Anti-Money Laundering.* Institute for International Economics, 2004.

Reuters. "IMF Aid for Seoul Rises, Humiliation Sinks In." December 4, Reuters. Available at: http://lists.jammed.com/IWAR/1997/12/0018.html, 1997.

Robinson, Roger W., Jr. "The National Security Dimensions of Global Capital Markets." May 7, William J. Casey Institute of the Center for Security Policy, 1999.

Rohter, Larry. "The Faraway War Set Latin America on Edge." *New York Times,* April 20, 2003.

Rose, Andrew K. "The Effect of Common Currencies on International Trade: Where Do We Stand?" Available at: http://faculty.haas.berkeley.edu/arose/MASOP02.pdf, 2002.

Roth, Stanley O. "Prepared Statement of Stanley O. Roth." May 7, Federal News Service, 1998.

Roubini, Nouriel, and Brad Setser. *Bailouts or Bail-Ins: Responding to Financial Crises in Emerging Markets.* Washington: Institute for International Economics, 2004.

Rubin, Robert E., Peter R. Orszag, and Allen Sinai. "Sustained Budget Deficits: Longer-Run U. S. Economic Performance and the Risk of Fiancial and Fiscal Disarray." January 4, Paper presented at the AEA-NAEFA Joint Session, Allied Social Science Association's Annual Meetings, January 4, 2004, 2004.

Rubin, Robert E., and Jacob Weisberg. *In an Uncertain World: Tough Choices from Wall Street to Washington.* New York: Random House, 2003.

Sachs, Jeffrey. "Managing the LDC Debt Crisis." *Brookings Papers on Economic Activity,* Issue 2, 1986.

Salvatore, Dominick. "Which Countries in the Americas Should Dollarize?" In Dominick Salvatore, James W. Dean, and Thomas Willett, eds., *The Dollarization Debate,* pp. 196–205. New York: Oxford University Press, 2003.

Sanger, David E. "Bailout of South Korea Raises Stakes for U.S." *New York Times,* November 22, 1997.

Scott Tyson, Ann. "Philippines Deployment: Sign of US Resolve." *Christian Science Monitor,* January 2, 2002.

Seidman, L. William. *Full Faith and Credit: The Great S&L Debacle and Other Washington Sagas.* District of Columbia: Beard Books, 1989.

Senate Banking, Housing and Urban Affairs Committee. "Hearing of the Senate Banking, Housing & Urban Affairs Committee: Federal Reserve Monetary Policy Report." July 20, Federal News Service, 2000

Shadow Financial Regulatory Committee. *Reforming Bank Capital Regulation.* Washington: AEI Press, 2000.

Simon, Sheldon. "The Economic Crisis and ASEAN States' Security." October 23, Strategic Studies Institute monograph, 1998.

Simpson, Glenn R. "As Investigations Proliferate, Big Banks Feel Under the Gun." *Wall Street Journal,* December 30, 2004.

Smead, Stuart W. "A Thesis on Maritime Piracy." Available at: http://www.angelfire.com/ga3/tropicalguy/piracy-modernday.html, 2001.

Snyder, Scott, and Richard H. Solomon. "Beyond the Asian Financial Crisis: Challenges and Opportunities for U.S. Leadership." April, United States Institute of Peace, Special Report 29, 1998.

Solomon, Gerald B. H. "Prepared Testimony by Congressman Gerald B. H. Solomon before the Senate Banking, Housing and Urban Affairs Committee, Financial Institutions and Regulatory Relief Subcommittee, Subject: U.S. Market Security Act." November 5, Federal News Service, 1997.

Spiro, David E. *Petrodollar Recycling and International Markets: The Hidden Hand of American Hegemony.* Ithaca: Cornell University Press, 1999.

Steil, Benn. "Enron and Italy: Parallels between Rome's Efforts to Qualify for Euro Entry and the Financial Chicanery in Texas." *Financial Times,* February 21, 2002.

———. "Whither International Regulation?" Unpublished presentation to the XIXth Annual Conference of the International Organization of Securities Commissions, October 17–21, 1994 (Tokyo, Japan).

Stratfor. "Latin America—Benign Neglect and Persistent Weakness." June 16, Stratfor, 2003.

Sulling, Anne. "Should Estonia Euroize?" *Economics of Transition* 10, no. 2 (2002): 469–90.

Summers, Lawrence. "Rules, Real Exchange Rates, and Monetary Discipline." In Nissan Liviatan, ed., *Proceedings of a Conference on Currency Boards and Currency Substitution,* pp. 32–33. Washington: World Bank, 1992.

Swindell, Bill. "Bush Caught Between Pakistan and Congress on Textile Imports." *Congressional Quarterly,* February 12, 2002.

Tarullo, Daniel K. *Banking on Basel: The Future of International Financial Regulation.* Institute for International Economics, Forthcoming

Thompson, Fred. "Senator Thompson Revises China Nonproliferation Act." July 26, Office of International Information Programs, U.S. Department of State, 2000.

Trinkunas, Harold, and Jack Boureston. "Financial and Political Crisis in Argentina: Walking a Wobbly Tightrope." *Strategic Insights* 1, no. 1 (March 2002).

Truman, Edwin. "Text: Assistant Secretary of Treasury Truman on Dollarization." Available at: http://www.usembassy.it/file2000_02/alia/a0020822.htm, 2000.

U.S. Senate Committee on Foreign Relations, Subcommittee on Foreign Relations. *International Debt, the Banks and U.S. Foreign Policy.* 95th Congress, First Session, 1977.

Unger, Laura S. "Letter to The Honorable Frank P. Wolf." In U.S.–China Security Review Commission, *Report to Congress of the U.S. China Security Review Commission,* July, pp. A28–A32, 2002.

United Nations Development Program. *Democracy in Latin America.* United Nations Development Program, 2004.

United States General Accounting Office. *Combating Money Laundering.* September 2003.

Vick, Karl. "Activists in Sudan Fear Loss of Western Oil Firms' Influence." *Washington Post,* June 24, 2001.

von Furstenberg, George M. "Pressures for Currency Consolidation in Insurance and Finance: Are the Currencies of Financially Small Countries on the Endangered List?" In Dominick Salvatore, James W. Dean, and Thomas Willett, eds., *The Dollarization Debate,* pp. 206–20. New York: Oxford University Press, 2003.

Wall Street Journal. "LDC Debt: To Worry or Not to Worry?" *Wall Street Journal,* January 23, pp. 25–28, 1981.

Wallich, Henry C. "LDC Debt: To Worry or Not to Worry?" *Challenge,* September/October, pp. 8–14, 1981.

Wechsler, William. "Follow the Money." *Foreign Affairs* 80, no. 4 (July/August 2001): 40–57.

Weiss, Martin. *Terrorist Financing: The 9/11 Commission Recommendation.* October, Congressional Research Service, 2004.

White, Michelle J. "Sovereigns in Distress: Do They Need Bankruptcy?" *Brookings Papers on Economic Activity,* issue 1 (2001): 287–319.

William J. Casey Institute of the Center for Security Policy. "Frank Wolf Puts U.S. Financial Regulators on Notice: Ignore U.S. Capital Market Fundraising for Sudan's Oil at Their Peril." March 16, William J. Casey Institute of the Center for Security Policy. Available at: http://www.centerforsecurity policy.org/index.jsp?section= papers&code=01-F_20, 2001.

Williams, Phil. "Drugs and Guns." *Bulletin of the Atomic Scientists* 55, no. 1 (January/February 1999).

Wishart, Eric. "Intelligence Networks and the Tri Border Area of South America: The Dilemma of Efficiency Versus Oversight." December, Thesis, Naval Postgraduate School, Monterey, California, 2002.

Wolf, Martin. "The Fund Is Not Equal to the Job It Was Meant to Do." *Financial Times,* March 10, 2004a.

———. *Why Globalization Works.* New Haven: Yale University Press, 2004b.

Worrell, DeLisle, and Hyginus Leon. "Price Volatility and Financial Instability." IMF Working Paper no. 01/60, 2001.

Wriston, Walter. "Banking Against Disaster." *New York Times,* September 14, 1982.

Zagaris, Bruce. "U.S. SEC Forms New Office of Global Security Risk." *International Enforcement Law Reporter,* April 2004.

INDEX

Afghanistan, 36
AFL-CIO, 58–59, 70, 77, 173n27
Al Qaeda, 40, 96. *See also* Jemaah Islamiyah
Albright, Madeleine, 57–58, 138
American Samoa, 128 (table)
AML. *See* anti–money laundering (AML) efforts
Andorra, 129 (table)
anti–money laundering (AML) efforts, 31; effectiveness, 32; future of, 160–61; improving, 44–47; international cooperation, 35–39, 171n15; knowing the customer, 34, 37–38, 42, 170nn5–6; limitations, 39–41, 171n19; list checking, 34–35, 39, 45, 170n7; Patriot Act provisions, 33, 34, 37–38; reporting transactions, 33–34, 37, 39–40; *See also* war on terror, finance and
anti-Americanism, 84–86, 93–94
Argentina: capital flows, 106; currency board unsuccessful, 127; financial crisis (1990s–2000s), 93–94, 96, 98, 119, 120 (figure), 142–43, 145; forced conversions, 127; IMF loans, 94, 145, 146; interest rates on Argentine deposits, 119, 120 (figure); seigniorage, 124

ASEAN (Association of Southeast Asian Nations), 87, 88, 155
Asia: bank bailouts, 123; multinational currency, 155; regional tensions, 86–88, 89; reserves and currency stability, 118; terrorism and terrorists, 41, 88–90. *See also* Asian financial crisis; *and specific countries*
Asian financial crisis, 82–90; anti-Americanism resulting from, 84–86; capital controls and, 29; effects, 81, 82, 84, 86–90; pegged exchange rate regimes unsuccessful in avoiding, 119; symptoms and causes, 83–84, 101–2, 104; U.S. foreign policy and, 138–41. *See also specific countries*
assets, freezing of, 36, 37, 171n13
Association of Southeast Asian Nations. *See* ASEAN
Australia–U.S. Free Trade Agreement, 170n42
Australian territories, 129 (table)

Bachus, Spencer, 65
Bahrain, 39, 155
Baldwin, David, 1
Bali terrorist bombings, 41, 90
Bank of England, 18
Bank Secrecy Act (BSA; U.S., 1970), 33